"THE WOMEN DIDN'T SEEM TO HAVE THE FIRST BIT OF MATERNAL INSTINCT."

CONTENTS.

LIST OF ILLUSTRATIONS.

CHAPTER I.

THE WILD MAN OF BORNEO.

How I became acquainted with the door-keeper is of no consequence. He assisted me to pass away several weary hours that I once spent in Chicago. I know very well that they ought not to have been weary hours. I should have visited the pork-packing establishments, and gazed at and duly admired the fifteen-and twenty-storey buildings that Chicago will con-

1

tinue to pride herself upon until an earthquake comes and convinces the occupants of the upper storeys that it would have been better for them if they had never been born.   It happened, however, that I was snowbound, and waiting until the snow-ploughs should succeed in opening the way for the transcontinental trains.   Being thus compelled to wait against my will, I was discontented, and took no delight in pork or tall buildings.   It was in these circumstances that I met the door-keeper, and found him to be, in the words of the landlord of my hotel : " One of the nicest gentlemen and spryest fighters in all Chicago ".

The door-keeper was the chief owner and manager of a Dime Museum.   The American Dime Museum does not bear the most distant resemblance to the British Museum.   It is simply an exhibition of monstrosities, genuine and artificial, and the public is admitted to view them on payment of a dime. These monstrosities, known in the " profession " as " freaks," seem to be produced in quantities to supply the demand.   Every Dime Museum professes to have the tallest giant, the smallest dwarf, the fattest fat woman, and the most beautiful Circassian girl in existence.   There are three or four Dime Museums in every city in the United States, not to speak of those that are on the road. How they all manage to find the necessary stock of genuine "freaks" is a mystery which the outside public cannot solve.

My door-keeper was, as I have said, the proprietor of his museum, but he occupied the post of door-keeper for the reason that he could thus make sure of receiving the money paid for admission, and, being a powerfully built man, could prevent the entrance of disorderly persons, and thus preserve the reputation of his museum as an "unequalled family resort," a claim made for it by the handbills. He loved to talk of his professional experiences, and in unfolding to me the private life of his "freaks" he opened up a new world. This is the story he told me concerning his "Wild Man of Borneo".

"Yes, sir! As I was saying, managing a company of 'freaks' ain't no picnic. They're the most quarrelsome lot that was ever got together outside of a meeting of politicians who want to bring about harmony in the party. A Fat Woman puts on more airs than any two Eyetalian primy-donners, and for bad temper there is nothing that can touch a Beautiful Circassian Girl. I have to spend about one-third of my time in keeping my

people from throwing crockery and pulling hair.
Except when they're falling in love, there ain't a
day that some one of them don't come to me and
swear that he or she'll leave if I don't discharge
some one else.

" Last year I had a Wild Man of Borneo who
was dead in love with the Tattooed Lady. It was
Barnum that invented the tattooed business, and for
a while it was the best line of business in the profession. Every museum was bound to have a Tattooed Girl, with a yarn about her having been
captured by the Indians and tattooed when she was
a little girl. My Circassian Girl jumped at the
chance of changing her line, for Circassian Girls
don't begin to draw as they did twenty years ago,
and when I proposed to her to do the Tattooed
Girl act, she set to work at once to draw patterns
for the tattooing, and being a mighty smart girl
she got up some of the best designs that I ever
saw.

" My Wild Man of Borneo was a thin, cadaver-
ous little chap, chock-full of sentiment and poetry
and all that sort of nonsense. When he got on his
paint, and danced his war-dance, and howled—in
what folks thought was the Borneo language—and
swallowed raw meat, you'd have thought that he

was about as murdering a style of savage as could be found, though he really wouldn't have hurt a fly. We kept him in a cage labelled 'Dangerous' until his part in the performance came round, and then a

THE WILD MAN OF BORNEO.

keeper would take him out and lead him with a chain around his waist to the platform, where he went through with his dancing and raw meat eating. I paid him a good salary, and he was worth it. I wish I had him back again in his cage. The

Wild Man I've got now is an Irishman, and he can't howl without a brogue that's bound to give him away some day.

" Now this Wild Man, the first one I mentioned, you understand, was the kind of chap that is always falling in love, and of course he fell in love with the Beautiful Circassian.   He wanted to marry her, and seeing as she didn't draw very well, and was getting tired of the business, and knowing that he was getting a good salary, and was a leading man in his line, she agreed to marry him.   I never liked the girl, for she was bad tempered and selfish, and I knew she didn't care a straw for the Wild Man, but I told her and him that if they'd wait six months I'd give them a bang-up wedding that shouldn't cost them a cent, and of course she insisted on waiting.

" When she went into the tattooed business, the Wild Man, being engaged to her, naturally insisted on doing the stencilling.   I know you won't give it away, so I don't mind telling you that the tattooing is put on every Monday with a stencil plate and brush, and is generally washed off on Saturday night when it begins to get faded.   It takes about two dozen different stencil plates to do a girl up in style, and give her a variety of patterns.

These plates were always kept in the property
room, and when Monday morning came around
the Wild Man would get them out and tattoo his
lady-love as gently as if he was a great artist,
painting a first-class, hand-made picture. He
took about twice as long as was necessary for

" STENCILLING."

the job, and I will say that when he was done,
he turned out the best Tattooed Girl that Chicago
ever saw.

" Well, one day I hired a Chinese Sword Swallower. He was a Frenchman, though I didn't
know it when I hired him. If I had, he would

never have come into my show, for a Frenchman is the most troublesome 'freak' in the whole profession, not excepting even the Dwarf, and he's, generally speaking, a holy terror. Naturally,

THE DWARF.

this Frenchman began to make love to the Tattooed Girl. I don't blame him for that, for, being a Frenchman, he had to act according to his nature; but he knew she was engaged to the Wild Man, and he had no business to meddle with an engaged girl, especially as there was the Fat Woman who hadn't anybody attached to her, and would have been thankful even for a Frenchman.

"Now this Sword Swallower was a rather handsome young fellow, with lots of swagger about him, and he gathered that Tattooed Girl in without the least trouble. She threw over the Wild Man, and wouldn't have anything more to do with him. She wouldn't even let him tattoo her, and said that the Sword Swallower was twice the artist that he was in handling a stencil brush. The poor chap came to me and said that he had made up his mind to commit suicide or to leave the business. He said that Jemima, for that was the girl's name, seemed to hate him. 'Once she used to admire me in my great meat-eating act,' said the Wild Man. 'Now she says that it is perfectly disgusting to eat raw meat, and she can't endure my black paint. She tells me that it's a low line of business to be a Wild Man, and that she thinks that sword swallowing is perfectly lovely. I say it ain't nothing of the sort. A sword ain't half as digestible as raw beef, and I don't care who says it is.'

"'You give her up, my boy,' I said. 'Don't waste your time over her. You're in the very front rank in your line, and that is something to be proud of.'

"'I know it,' said he; 'but I can't stay in this show if that Sword Swallower stays. My contract will be up next month, and you might as well let me off now. If you don't, there is nothing for me except the cold and silent grave.'

"'You drop that nonsense!' said I. 'The grave's no sort of place for a man of talent like you. Leave this business to me, and I promise you that inside of a week Jemima will give that Frenchman his walking ticket, and you'll have the field to yourself again.'

"He was a trusting little beggar, and had no end of confidence in me. What I said brought up his spirits again, and that afternoon he howled better than he had ever howled before, and two women fainted away when he jumped at them with his spear, as if he was going to run them through then and there.

"Now I happened to have a lot of stencil plates that I used to mark boxes with, and knowing that the Frenchman couldn't read or write, I felt pretty sure that I could put up a job on him that would settle his business with the Tattooed Girl. In the course of the day I took six of her stencil

plates out of the drawer where they were kept,
and put six of mine on the top of the pile in their

"TWO WOMEN FAINTED AWAY."

place, and waited for next Monday morning to
come round.

"Naturally it came round, and naturally the
Frenchman was on hand at eleven o'clock to stencil
the girl, so as to be ready for the afternoon exhibition. He never noticed any difference between
the plates he had been using and the ones I had
furnished, for besides not being able to read, he
was so taken up with making love to the girl,
that he never had no time to notice anything else.
It was the same way with her. She supposed

that the stencilling was going on all right, and she never so much as looked at the plates, knowing that the Frenchman always used them in regular order, beginning with the top of the pile.

"He always began with her back, and when he had used up six of the stencil plates, he had her shoulders and forehead stencilled, and then went to work on her neck. The plates he used for this part of his work were the regular ones, and as the girl couldn't see her forehead or her back, she supposed they were all right, which they wasn't, as you will presently understand.

"After the tattooing was over, and the Frenchman had gone to dinner, I took the girl into my office and kept her there till the performance began, so that nobody should be able to see her. While the show was going on she had to sit in a chair on a raised platform, where everybody could see her, and when her turn came the chair was slowly twisted round, while the lecturer told the yarn about her having been captured by Indians, and explained her diagrams. She couldn't help noticing that people stared at her more than usual when they came in, and she supposed that the stencilling must have been done extra particular well.

"What they were staring at, however, was her forehead, which was stencilled 'J. M. H.,' being my initials, and they naturally wondered how the Indians came to tattoo a girl with English letters. But it was when the lecturer began to explain her,

" HOW THEY CHAFFED THAT POOR GIRL ! "

and turned her chair round so as to show her back, that the fun began. Across the back of her neck was ' Keep Dry,' in big letters; a little farther down was 'Very Fragile,' and 'Handle With Care'. One arm was marked 'Strictly Private,'

and the other 'This Side Up,' and, as good luck
would have it, the Frenchman had not got a single
plate upside down.

"Well, when the people saw it, they first
laughed themselves sick, and then got mad. They
said they had been swindled, and that the girl
had never been near no Indians. One fellow said
that seeing as she wasn't a leopard she couldn't
change her own spots, and that, consequently, I
had changed them for her, and was a thief and
an impostor. And how they chaffed that poor
girl! I really felt sorry for her, though I knew
she deserved it all. As for the lecturer, he left
as soon as the first egg hit him on the head, and
the girl would have left too, if she had been able
to get out of the crowd.

"I let the row run along a little in hopes that
the Frenchman would get mixed up in it, but he
was no such man, and he bolted the minute it began.
So seeing as there was danger that the crowd
would wreck the establishment, I went in with
three policemen and my four teamsters, and we
cleared out the people without much trouble. I
told them that there had been a mistake, and that
the Tattooed Girl being sick couldn't show that day,
and my secretary, not wishing to disappoint the

people, had got a substitute without consulting me. What with offering them free tickets for the next day, and licking half a dozen or so of the most cheeky, I settled the affair up, and the next day the show was as peaceful as ever.

"SHE WOULD TEAR HIS EYES OUT."

"What became of the Wild Man! Oh! I 'most forgot to tell you. When the Tattooed Girl found out what the row had been about, she swore that the Frenchman had done it on purpose, and that she would never see him again, barring such time as might be necessary to tear his eyes out. He heard of this, and had sense enough to keep on his side of the house, and she never had a chance to get at his eyes. After the month was up he left me, and that was the last I ever saw of him. The field being clear, the Wild Man makes up to the girl again, and she takes him back, making it a condition, however, that he should give up the Wild Man business, and go into some other. So he set to work, and learned the sword swallowing act, though a Sword Swallower doesn't

THE CHINESE SWORD SWALLOWER. command more than half the average wages of a first-class Wild Man. He's doing sword swallowing in my museum now, and don't like it very much. He told me the other day that he hankered for his old life. ' Thishyer

swallowing business is too conventional for me,'
he said. 'There ain't no room for the display of
histrionic talent, like there was in that raw meat act.
But she won't have it, and I must do what pleases
her.'

"They calculate to be married in about two
months, and then I'll lose them both, for of course
they'll quarrel, so that I shall have to get rid of the
pair of them. Well, it was what might have been
expected, after letting a Frenchman into the show.
If it wasn't that she is a mighty handsome woman,
and has got the best stencilling in the profession,
I'd bribe her to leave on the sly, and I'd get her
lover to go back to the Wild Man business. It's
the only line fit for a man of his talent, and he's
just throwing himself away, as you might say, now
that he's only a Chinese Sword Swallower."

CHAPTER II.

A GORILLA ROMANCE.

THE door-keeper threw himself into one of the large arm-chairs of the smoking-room of the Potter

House, which, as every one knows, is the chief
hotel of Chicago, and one of the objects of which no
stranger can speak disrespectfully to a Chicago man
and live. He wiped his brow with his enormous
yellow silk handkerchief, and ordered the waiter to
bring him some whisky. As he was ordinarily a
total abstainer, it was evident that something
very unusual had happened to disturb the even
current of his habits, and I asked him what was
the matter.

" If you'd been up to my museum an hour ago,
you wouldn't have asked what was the matter.
You'd have seen for yourself the biggest row I've
struck since I've been running a Dime Museum in
this town, and I've been here now going on five
years."

" How did it happen ? " I asked.

" It didn't happen.   It was the natural consequence of my cussed soft-heartedness.   That's
what's stood in my light ever since I went into
business for myself.   Never you do a kind action :
that is, unless you're a millionaire, and don't have
to depend on your own exertions for a living.
What's that song the Sunday-school children
sing ? ' Kind words can never die ! ' That's just
what's the matter with them. They keep alive,

and keep a-getting even with you all the rest of
your life. Why, I'd have been a rich man twenty
times over, if I had sense enough to be a little less
darned benevolent.

"About three weeks ago, a chap from California
—so he said—came to see me in my office, and
wanted a situation as a Gorilla. He was ragged
and thin, and said that he was starving. When I
asked him if he'd had any experience as a Gorilla,
he was honest enough to say that he hadn't, but he
said he had been a conductor on a Chicago street
car, and he calculated that the Gorilla business
would come middling easy to him. Well! I
couldn't help feeling sorry for him, and then I knew
that a good Gorilla is one of the strongest attractions a Dime Museum can have. I hadn't any
Gorilla, for the last one I had died of delirium
tremens, and I was waiting till I could find one
who was a Blue Ribbon man. I asked the man if
he was a steady drinker, or only a periodical drinker,
and he swore that he had never touched a drop of
whisky in his life, and had a medal at the pawn-
broker's that John B. Gough had hung around his
neck with his own hands. I was fool enough to
believe this, though I know as well as anybody else
that a Californian who says he never drinks is only

saving up his thirst till it gets good and strong, and
then just you look out for him.   I hired that fellow
then and there, and had him measured for a suit of
Gorilla skins that very afternoon.

"THE STRONGEST WOMAN IN THE WORLD."

" He took to the business quite naturally, and
as I had a good, comfortable cage made for him, he
led a pretty easy life.   He enjoyed pulling off the

women's bonnets when they came too near his cage,
and the other women who had the sense to keep
outside of his reach said it was just too sweet for
anything to see the solemn way in which the poor
dear beast would sit and pull those vulgar, ridiculous bonnets to pieces.   After the show closed, and
the Gorilla had got his skin off, and washed the
paint off his face and hands, he would sit down with
the other Freaks, and make himself generally popular, being in the main a good-tempered chap, with
a lot of good stories, and two or three pretty good
songs.

"There was one of our company that didn't like
the Gorilla, and nothing he could do would make
her admit that there was any good in him.   This
was the Combined Female Contortionist and Strongest Woman in the World.   She was genuine, and
corresponded in every particular to the small bills,
which is more than you can rightly expect in any
show.   To see her standing on her head and balancing the Dwarf on one foot, and the Living Skeleton
on the other, was a sight to draw tears from the
eyes of any one that knows what real genius is.
Then you should have seen her hold the Fat
Woman in her teeth.   She would stand on a raised
platform, and after a belt was fastened round the

Fat Woman's waist, she would take it in her teeth
and swing her clear of the floor. ·The Fat Woman's
weight was genuine, too, for she wore a lead corset
to bring her up to seven hundred pounds, she being
naturally plump, and weighing a good one hundred
and fifty without her pads and her corset. She was
a good girl, too, was the Strongest Woman, and
her whole soul was in her profession. She didn't
want to get married nor any such nonsense, and
she used to say that she had rather be able to
balance the Fat Woman on her feet, she standing
on her head at the time, than to be married to Jay
Gould, and have him die the next day. That was
what she was trying to work up to, you understand
—the balancing of the Fat Woman on both feet—
same as she balanced the Dwarf and the Living
Skeleton ; and I believe that she would have fetched
it in time. What she will do now nobody knows,
and he won't tell.

" The Living Skeleton had never seemed to care
for anything but his meals, he being a most tremendous eater, like most of his sort. That's the
way Living Skeletons are educated. Feed them on
nothing but meat, and keep feeding them about once
in every three hours, and you'll turn out as many
Living Skeletons as the market can hold, He had

been with me going on for seven years, and had never showed the least grain of interest in any woman; but his time had come at last.   He fell in love with the Strongest Woman, and he had it mighty bad. 'It's all on account of that balancing act,' he said to me. 'The very first time I sat on the sole of her foot and she stood on her head, so calm and sweet and like a first-class regular angel, I knew it was all up with me.   I don't care for my meals no more compared with what I used to, and if I can't win her love, I know I shall grow fat and choke to death, like that genuine Fat Boy we had last year.'

" I tried to get at the Strongest Woman's views about the Skeleton, and I didn't have much difficulty about it.   She said he was a nice, quiet, gentlemanly person, and if she was a marrying woman she might think seriously about him.

"'As it is,' she said, 'I am wedded to my profession, and I won't marry any man, at least not while I am before the public.   I'll be a sister to him, if that'll suit him, but he had better forget me, and take care of himself.   I'm very much afraid it is telling on him, and he is gaining flesh.'

" Now the Gorilla, being sweet on the Strongest Woman himself, and she hating him as the devil

"THE GORILLA WAS ALWAYS SAYING AGGRAVATING THINGS TO THE SKELETON."

does soda-water, as the saying is, grew sulky. He took to getting angry at what the public said about him, and when a man would say, 'What a horrid ugly beast he is, to be sure,' the Gorilla would want to talk back at him, though, of course, he had sense enough not to do it. However, I began to get uneasy, for I was afraid that the Gorilla would take to drink, and do something that would create a scandal, or that he would break out into language, and slang the public till they would lose confidence not only in him, but in all the rest of the show. The Fat Woman, who sat next to him at table, was a good deal worried too, for she was afraid of him, and as she afterwards told me, was always expecting to see him try to ease his mind on the Living Skeleton, of whom he was naturally jealous. The poor woman, who was as kind-hearted a soul as ever lived, was so taken up with the affair that she could think of nothing else, and often she would forget to scream when a boy would stick a pin into her ankle, which, of course, led to doubts as to her genuineness.

"The Gorilla was always saying aggravating things to the Skeleton ; which was contemptible, seeing as the Skeleton was as weak as a cat and had nothing of the fighting man about him. When

I overheard anything of the kind, I, of course, gave
the Gorilla my views on his conduct, and warned
him that I would discharge him if he made trouble
in my Happy Family; but for all that I saw the
day was coming when he would be sure to break
out, and I more than half made up my mind to discharge him without waiting for any outbreak.   But
there again my cussed benevolence stood in my
way, and I couldn't quite bring myself to discharge
a really efficient Gorilla just because he didn't happen
to like the Living Skeleton.   Well, the crisis was
bound to come, as a crisis always does, except, of
course, when it has something to do with politics.
This morning the Gorilla went out early and bought a
bottle of whisky and smuggled it into his cage, where
he hid it under the straw.   He would go and take
a hack at it every half-hour or so, and when the
show opened he was about as full as he could hold.

" At first the public didn't notice anything pecu-
liar, and probably thought that the Gorilla had been
fed pretty well, and was in unusually good spirits.
The fact was that he was fighting drunk, and was
cussin' the public to himself in a way that would
have led to somebody's getting insulted and drawing on him if he had been understood.   By-and-by
a fat, big, stupid-looking politician came along, and,

after standing a while in front of the Gorilla's cage, remarked to a friend that the Gorilla was almost as ugly as a nigger, and he wondered he didn't have a place on the Republican General Committee. The Gorilla happened to be a Democrat of the p'isonest kind, and to be compared to a nigger, and called a Republican all at once, was more than he could stand. He shook his fist through the bars of his cage at the man and said: ' Look here! If you're man enough to take off your coat, I'll smash the ugly face off you with all the pleasure in life! ' The man was so much astonished to hear the Gorilla speak that at first it took his breath away, but being a fighter from way back, as an active politician has got to be, he said after a minute: ' Come out of that cage, you dirty beast, and we'll see who is the better man '. With that the Gorilla threw away the stick he always carried, pretending that he needed it to help him stand upright, and opened the door of his cage and jumped down.

" I wasn't there at the start, and they tell me that I missed one of the prettiest fights that Chicago ever saw. The politician kept his end up middling well, but the Gorilla was too much for him, and in three rounds knocked him clean out. By that time the excitement was tremendous: the women were

screaming and fainting and making for the door all
at once, and the men were trying to get in the front
of the ring, and betting on the Gorilla or the politician, according as their best judgment dictated,
and yelling with as much enthusiasm as if they
were attending a political convention.　When the
Gorilla had finished his man he asked if any other
gentleman would like to step forward, but nobody
seemed to want to take a hand, so the Gorilla
judged that the time had come for him to attend to
his private interests, and get square with the Living Skeleton.　He made straight for the platform
where the Freaks were sitting, and went for that
Skeleton as if there were no hereafter for either of
them.　After he had offered to knock the Skeleton's
head off for two cents, and had his offer declined,
he reached for him, but the Fat Woman gave a
shriek, and waddling between them fell on the
Gorilla and floored him.　The crowd cheered, and
for a minute the betting on the Fat Woman and the
Gorilla was about even, but he managed to get on
his feet again, and, owing to the Fat Woman's having torn a hole in her stocking during the struggle,
her bran began to flow, and before she could get to
the dressing room she was reduced to her natural
size, and her reputation was gone for ever.

" The coast being now clear, the Gorilla grabbed the Skeleton by the waistband, and was going to heave him clean across the room, when the Strongest Woman walks up to him, and without saying a word, gives him one in the right eye, straight from the shoulder. It knocked him off the

" A MOST ASTONISHED GORILLA."

platform, and when he pulled himself together and got on his legs again he was the most astonished Gorilla you ever dreamed of. However, seeing as he was fighting drunk, he wasn't going to be contented with one flooring. He climbed on the platform again and went for the Skeleton a second time,

but the Strongest Woman was there before him.
She took him by the collar of his skin and his right
leg, and giving him a gentle swing, so as to get the
heft·of him, you understand, she hove him about
thirty feet straight through the air.   He brought up
against the side of his cage, and when some gentlemen, desiring to see the thing out, picked him up
and sponged him off, he said he had had enough.
About half of his ribs, I should judge, was stove in,
and he's in the hospital this very minute.

   " I arrived just as they were picking him up, and
as soon as I knew how things stood I made the
people a speech.   I asked them if, as honest men
and gentlemen, they could deny that they had their
full money's worth ; and they owned that they had.
I said: ' Gentlemen! there's tricks in every trade,
and I don't pretend to say that my Gorilla and my
Fat Woman are not to a certain extent works of art.
But tell me in what other show you ever saw such
a heavenly fight, and such a magnificent display of
the beauty, nobility, and purity of woman ? '

   " Well, they were pretty middling sensible people,
I will give them that much credit, and they agreed
that they had no reason to be dissatisfied, and after
talking the fight over for a while, and taking up a
collection for the Strongest Woman, which panned

out more than thirty dollars, they left, giving three
cheers for the Strongest Woman and for me.

"I consider that I am well out of a bad scrape,

but for all that my losses this day have been pretty
heavy. I've lost my Gorilla, and, what is worse,
the public has lost confidence in Gorillas, and I
shan't be able to exhibit another for at least a year.

3

Then the Fat Woman's reputation is gone, and she
can never show again in Chicago until people have
forgotten her and she has changed her name. Besides, I shall have to get a genuine Fat Woman to
take her place, and they come high, there not being
enough of them to supply the demand. Taking one
thing with another, I calculate that this day's work
will cost me, in the course of the year, not less than
three hundred dollars, not including the cost of
burying the Gorilla's remains, if it comes to that,
as it probably will. If ever you go into the show
business, you take my advice and never have anything to do with an American Gorilla, no matter
what State he comes from. Get a good sober
German. They make the best and the most reli-
able Gorillas in the profession."

CHAPTER III.

MAJOR MICROBE.

" I'VE been in the show business now going on for forty-three years," said the door-keeper, "and I haven't yet found a Dwarf with human feelings. I can't understand why it is, but there ain't the least manner of doubt that a Dwarf is the meanest object in creation. Take General Bacillus, the Dwarf I have with me now. He is well made, for a Dwarf, and when he does his poses plastic, such as 'Ajax Defying the Lightning,' or 'Samson Carrying off Delilah by the Hair,' and all the rest of those Scripture tablows, he is as pretty as a picture, provided, of course, you don't get too near him. He is healthy and has a good appetite, and he draws a good salary, and has no one except himself to look after. And yet that Dwarf ain't happy! On the contrary, he is the most discontented, cantankerous, malicious little wretch that was ever admitted into a Moral Family Show. And he ain't much worse than an ordinary Dwarf. Now, the other Freaks, as a rule,

(33)

are contented so long as they draw well, and don't fall in love.

" The Living Skeleton knows that he can't expect to live long—most of them die at about thirty-five— but, for all that, he is happy and contented. 'A short life and a merry one is what I goes in for,' he often says to me, and he seems to think that his life is a merry one, though I can't myself see where the merriment comes in.   So with all the rest of my people.   They all seem to enjoy themselves except the Dwarf.   My own belief is that the organ of happiness has got to be pretty big to get its work in, and that there ain't room in a Dwarf's head for it to work.

" I had a Dwarf with me once—Major Microbe is what we called him on the bills, where he was advertised as the 'Smallest Man in the World,' which, of course, he wasn't; but, then, every Dwarf is always advertised that way.   It's a custom of the profession, and we don't consider it to be lying, any more than a President considers the tough state-ments lying that he makes in his annual message. A showman and a politician must be allowed a little liberty of statement, or they couldn't carry on their business.   Well, as I was saying, thishyer Major Microbe was in my show a matter of ten years ago,

when we were in Cincinnati, and he was about as
vicious as they make them. The Giant, who was
a good seven-footer, working up to seven and a
half feet, as an engineer might say, with the help
of his boots and helmet, was the exact opposite of
the Dwarf in disposition. He was altogether too
good-tempered, for he was always trying to play
practical jokes on the other Freaks. He did this
without any notion of annoying them, but it was
injudicious; he being, like all other Giants, weak
and brittle.

"What do I mean by brittle? Why, I mean
brittle and nothing else. It's a good United
States word, I reckon. Thishyer Giant's bones
weren't made of the proper materials, and they were
always liable to break. He had to take the greatest
care of himself, and to avoid arguing on politics or
religion or anything like that, for a kick on the shins
would be sure to break one of his legs, which would
lay him on the shelf for a couple of months. As
for his arms, he was for ever breaking one or two of
them, but that didn't so much matter, for he could
go on the stage with his arm in splints and a sling,
and the public always supposed that he was repre-
senting a heroic soldier who had just returned from
the battle-field.

"One day the Giant put up a job on the Dwarf
that afterwards got them both into serious trouble.

"The Giant was loafing around the place after
dinner, and he found the Dwarf asleep on a bench.
What does he do but cover him up. with a rug and
then go off in search of the Fat Woman, who was a
sure enough Fat Woman, and weighed in private
life four hundred and nineteen pounds. The Giant
was popular with the sex, and the Fat Woman was
glad to accept his invitation to come with him and
listen to a scheme that he pretended to have for in-
creasing the attractions of Fat Women. He led her
up to where the Dwarf was asleep on the bench and
invited her to sit down, saying that he had arranged
a cushion for her to make her comfortable. Of
course she sat down, and sat down pretty solid too,
directly on the Dwarf. The Dwarf yelled as if he
had room for the voice of two full-grown men, and
the Fat Woman, as soon as she felt something
squirming under her, thought that one of the boa
constrictors had got loose, and that she had sat
down on it. So naturally she fainted away. I came
running in with one of my men as soon as I heard
the outcries, and after a while we managed to pry
up the Fat Women with a couple of cart-rungs and
get the Dwarf out from under her, after which she

"HE FOUND THE DWARF ASLEEP ON A BENCH."

came to in due time and got over her fright. But
the Dwarf was a good deal flattened out by the pres-
sure, and I was afraid at first that his ribs had been
stove in. It turned out in the end that he was not
seriously injured; but he was in the worst rage against
the Giant that you can imagine, and would have
killed him then and there if he had been able to do it.

" I knew well enough that in course of time the
Dwarf would get square with the Giant, no matter
how long it might take and how much it might cost.
He was as revengeful as a Red Indian. I warned
the Giant that he must keep a sharp look-out, or the
Dwarf would do him a mischief; but he said ' he
calculated he was big enough to take care of himself, and that he wasn't afraid of no two-foot Dwarf
that ever breathed '. Of course, this sounded brave,
but my own belief is that the Giant was pretty badly
frightened. I noticed that he never allowed himself
to be alone with the Dwarf, and was always careful to mind where he stepped, so as not to get tripped
up by strings stretched across the path, or anything
of that sort. The Dwarf pretended that he had forgotten the whole business, and was as friendly with
the Giant as he had ever been; but I knew him well
enough to know that he never forgot anything, and
was only waiting for a chance.

" Pretty soon little accidents began to happen to
the Giant.   One day he would find that his helmet,
which was made of pasteboard, had fallen into a tub

"HIS HELMET HAD FALLEN INTO A TUB OF WATER."

of water, and gone to everlasting jelly.   This would
oblige him to show himself bare-headed, which took
off several inches from his professional height.

Another day his boots would be in the tub, and he wouldn't be able to get them on. I've seen him go on the stage in a general's uniform with carpet slippers and no hat, which every one knew must be contrary to the regulations of the Arabian army, in which he was supposed to hold his commission.

" One night his bedstead broke down under him, and he came very near breaking a leg or so. In the morning he found out that some one had sawed a leg of the bedstead nearly all the way through, and, of course, he knew that the Dwarf had done it. But you couldn't prove anything against the Dwarf. He would always swear that he never had any hand in the accidents, and there was never any evidence against him that anybody could get hold of. I didn't mind what games he played on the Giant as long as the Giant wasn't made to break anything that would lay him on the shelf, and I told the Dwarf that I was the last man to interfere with any man's innocent amusements, but that in case the Giant happened to break a leg, I should go out of the Giant and Dwarf business at once. But that didn't scare him a particle. He knew that he was worth his salary in any Dime Museum in America, and more than that, he had money enough laid up in the bank to live on, assuming, of course, that he

could draw it out before the cashier should bolt to
Canada with it.   So he was as independent as you
please, and told me that if I chose to hold him re-
sponsible for other people's legs he couldn't help it,
and had nothing to say about it.

"At that time I had a Female Samson.   She
wasn't the Combined Female Contortionist and
Strongest Woman in the World that is in my show
at present, but she was in about the same line of
business.   These Strong Women are all genuine,
you understand.   You can embellish them a little
on the handbills, and you can announce that the
cannon that the Strong Woman fires from her
shoulder weighs a hundred or two pounds more
than it actually weighs; but unless a Strong
Woman is really strong and no mistake, she might
as well try to pass herself off as a Living Skeleton
or a Two-Headed Girl at once.   The fact is, the
great majority of Freaks are genuine, and the business is a thoroughly honest one at bottom.   Why,
if you told the exact truth in the handbills about
every Freak in my show, barring the Tattooed Girl
and the Wild Man, they would still constitute a
good drawing attraction in any intelligent community.

" This Female Samson was a good sort of

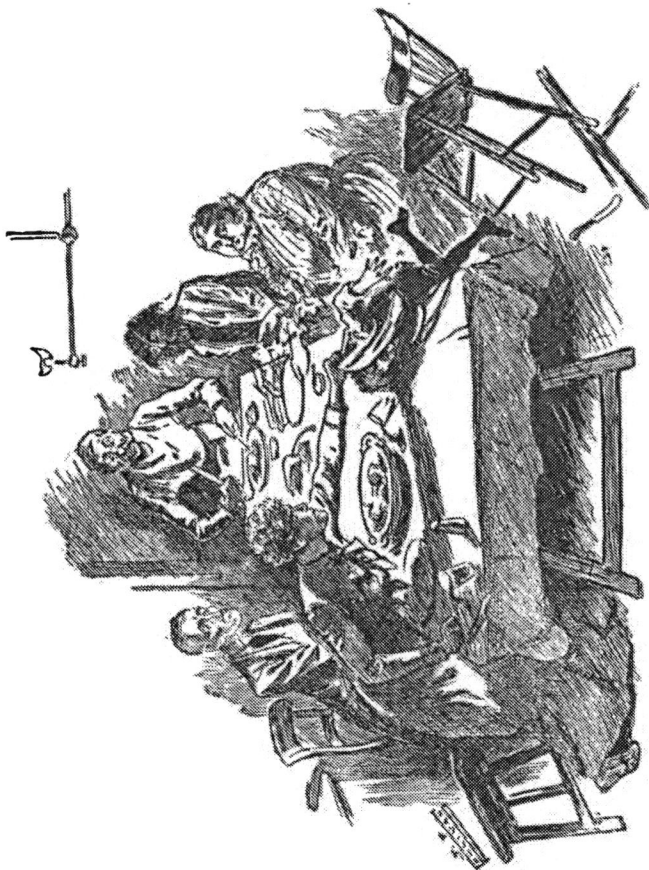

"SHE PULLED HIM OVER TO HER BY HIS COLLAR."

woman in her way, though she was a little rough and a bit what you might call masculine in her ways. She didn't like the Dwarf, and he didn't like her.

"The Freaks were all at supper one night when the Dwarf said something insulting to the Female Samson. He sat right opposite to her, and she just reached across the table and pulled him over to her by his collar. Then she stretched him across her lap and laid into him with her slipper till he howled as if he was a small boy who had gone in swimming on Sunday and his mother had just found it out. It wasn't so much the slipper that hurt him, though the Female Samson put all her muscle into the operation, but it was the disgrace of the thing; and when you remember that the Dwarf was forty-two years old, you can understand that he felt that the woman had taken a liberty with him. However, the next day he seemed to have forgotten all about it, and when the Giant reminded him of the circumstance, which he did every little while, the Dwarf would grin and say that we must let the women do what they liked, for they were a superior sort of being.

"One of the Female Samson's best feats was done in company with the Dwarf and the Giant.

She had a horizontal bar fixed on the stage, about
ten feet above the floor.   On this bar she used to
swing head downwards, just hooking her knees
around it, as all the trapeze artists do.   It looks
sort of uncomfortable, but it is nothing when you
are used to it.   I had a trapeze chap once who
would often go to sleep that way in hot weather.
He said that all the blood in his body went into his
head, and that made him feel sleepy, while it cooled
off his body and legs.   There's no accounting for
tastes, but as for me, give me a good bed where I
can stretch out, and I'll never ask to sleep on a
trapeze bar.

"As I was saying, the Female Samson would
swing on this bar, and then she would take the
Dwarf's belt in her teeth and hold him in that way
for five minutes.   There was a swivel in the belt,
so that the Dwarf would spin round while she was
holding him, which he didn't like much, but which
pleased the public.   After she had swung the Dwarf
she would do the same act with the Giant.   She had
to be very careful not to drop the Giant, for he was
terribly afraid of breaking a leg, being, as I have
said, particularly brittle; but she always said that
he was as safe in her teeth as he would be if he was
lying in his bed.

" It must have been about a fortnight after the
Dwarf was sat on by the Fat Woman, and a week
or more after he had been corrected in public by
the Female Samson, that we had an unusually
large evening audience, and everybody was in
excellent spirits. The Female Samson had swung
the Dwarf in her teeth, and after she had let go of
him he had climbed up on a chair just behind her,
and stood with his arms stretched out over her and
the Giant as if he was saying, ' Bless you, my
children,' which was a regular part of the act, and
never failed to bring him a round of applause, and
induce people to say, ' What a jolly little chap that
Dwarf is ! ' When the Female Samson had got a
good grip of the Giant's belt, and had raised him
about five feet from the floor, the Dwarf leaned a
little bit forward and ran a pin into the Female
Samson's ankle, or thereabouts. Nobody saw him
do it, but it was easy to prove it on him afterwards,
for he dropped the pin on the floor when he had
finally got through with it, and everybody recognised
it as one of his scarf-pins.

" The woman would naturally have shrieked
when she felt the pin, but she had her mouth
full of Giant, and she couldn't do more than
mumble a little in a half-smothered sort of way.

4

The Dwarf paid no attention to that, but gave her
another eye-opener with the pin. It went in about
an inch, judging from what the Female Samson
said when she described her sufferings, and it must
have hurt her pretty bad ; but she was full of pluck
and bound to carry out her performance to the end.
She stood three or four more prods, and then, not
being able to stand it any longer without express-
ing her feelings in some way, she unhooked one
leg and fetched the Dwarf a kick on the side of the
head that reminded him that it was about time for
him to get into his own room and lock the door,
and convinced him that there ain't a bit of ex-
aggeration in the tough stories that they tell about
the kicking powers of an army mule. The kick
sent the Dwarf clean across the platform, and the
people, not understanding the situation, began to
cry ' Shame '. Whether this flurried the Female
Samson or not, or whether she lost her balance
entirely on account of having unhooked one leg, I
don't know. What I do know is that she slipped
off the bar, and she and the Giant struck the floor
with a crash that would have broken the planks, if it
had not been that the platform was built expressly
to stand the strain of the Fat Woman.

" It wouldn't have been so bad if she had just

dropped the Giant, and hung on to the bar herself. In that case he would probably have broken his left leg and arm and collar bone, just as he did break them, but his ribs would have been all right. As it was, the Female Samson's head came down

"IT TOOK FOUR MEN AND A POLICEMAN TO HOLD HER."

just in the centre of him, and stove in about three-fourths of his ribs. She wasn't hurt at all, for, being a woman, and falling on her head, there was nothing for her to break, and the Giant was so soft that falling on him didn't even give her a headache.

When some volunteers from the audience had picked up the Giant and put him on a stretcher and carried him to the hospital, where the doctors did their best to mend him, the Female Samson had a

chance to explain, and the finding of a long scarf-pin on the platform, just under the bar, was evidence that she had told the truth, and corroborated the red stain on her stocking.

" It took four men and a policeman to hold her, and get her locked up in her room, she was that set on tearing the Dwarf into small pieces, and she'd have done it too, if she could have got at him. He had sense enough to see the situation, and to discharge himself without waiting for me to discharge him. He ran away in the course of the night, and I never saw him again. I don't think he ever went into another Dime Museum, and I have heard that he got a situation as inspector of gas meters, which is very probable, considering what a malicious little rascal he was. Well, we have to deal with all sorts of people in our business, and I suppose it's the same with you, though you haven't mentioned what your business is. But you take my advice and steer clear of Dwarfs. There ain't a man living that can do anything with them except with a club, and no man likes to take a club to anything as small as a Dwarf."

CHAPTER IV.

A CASE OF DUAL CONSCIOUSNESS.

"OF course," said the door-keeper, "we calculate, in the Dime Museum business, to deceive the public a little now and then, but as it is done for the amusement and instruction of the public, I don't see as any one has any call to complain. Suppose I do exhibit a 'freak' that isn't quite genuine! If it draws it is because the public likes it, in which case the public ought to be satisfied. If it doesn't draw, the public doesn't pay out any money to see it, and naturally doesn't feel that it is swindled. Now, I was swindled once, and pretty bad too, by an artificial 'freak,' and it was me and not the public that suffered. If you want to hear about it I'll tell you the whole story, though I shouldn't like it to be known in the profession, for it don't do any credit to me as a professional man.

" I was exhibiting in Boston a good many years ago, and I am free to say that I was losing money. Boston don't seem to care for natural 'freaks'. It goes in for philosophical and philanthropic 'freaks'. I've nothing against that style of 'freak' myself, but I claim that a genuine Giant, or a real Fat Woman, is just as improving, and a sight more interesting, than any philosopher or philanthropist that Boston ever produced.

"I don't like to lose money any more than you do, and things were looking pretty blue for me, when one day a carriage drives up to my door and a chap sends in word that he wanted to see me on professional business. I told my man to show him in, and when I saw him I put him down for a rascal without waiting to hear him speak. He told me that he had just arrived from Europe with a Two-Headed Girl, and that she was the biggest thing that any Museum had ever offered to the public. He had her with him in the carriage, and I was the first manager that he had called to see since he landed.

"Now I knew well enough that a Two-Headed Girl is about the scarcest thing that a Museum can get hold of. I never knew of but one specimen of the kind, and she was worth pretty near her weight in gold. How this fellow should have got hold of a second specimen without my ever having heard of her existence was more than I could understand, for I kept as bright a look-out for attractions all over the world as Barnum himself. However, I went out to the carriage and had a look at the girl. There she sat, wrapped up in a big shawl, and as far as I could see she was all right. Anyway, there were two heads above the edge of the shawl, and they were as pretty heads as you could find in any English young ladies' seminary. If the Two-Headed Girl only corresponded to the sample I saw in the carriage, she would be the biggest attraction that Boston or any other city had ever seen.

"Well! I went back to my office, and the fellow and I talked the thing over. He said the girl was a Laplander, and couldn't speak a single word of any language except Laplandish. She was sixteen years old, and had never been out of her native village until he had accidentally seen her, and hired her for a five years' tour of the world. So far he had not exhibited her anywhere, and he wanted her to make her deebutt in my show, so as to give her a respectable standing in the profession from the start. His terms were a hundred dollars a week, and a benefit every six months, and he said that he should ask any other manager a hundred and twenty-five.

" I told him to bring in his girl where I could
have a fair look at her, and then it would be time
enough to talk about terms.   He brought her in,
and I noticed that she climbed down out of the
carriage with considerable difficulty.   The agent

"SHE SMILED AT ME WITH BOTH HEADS."

helped her into my office, where she sat down on
the sofa, and smiled at me with both heads in a
way that would have been dangerous if she had
tried it on some managers that I know.

" 'There she is,' said the agent.   'The only

genuine white Two-Headed Girl the world has ever
seen.   Above the waist, where she is joined together, she is perfect : two distinct girls, and good-
looking ones too.   She's only got one pair of legs,
which prevents her from walking easy, but she is
as strong and healthy as they make 'em, and there
ain't the least danger that she'll die on your hands.'

"Then he spoke some gibberish, which I supposed was Laplandish, to the girl, and she drew up
the hem of her dress so as to show two nice little
feet, and no more.   The size of those feet ought to
have awakened my suspicion, for they were the
regulation Boston size, which is about three sizes
smaller than the average European foot.   But I
was so anxious to find that she was genuine that I
didn't notice that there was anything wrong about
her feet.

"'What do you say?' said the agent. 'Isn't
she a first-class attraction?'

"'She'll draw safe enough,' said I, 'provided
she's genuine.   I don't mean to say she ain't, but
I've got to be sure about it before we can do any
business.'

"'Oh! It's easy enough to prove that she is
genuine,' says the fellow. 'I've got certificates
from three of the leading physicians in Lapland,

besides the affidavit of her father and mother and the parish priest. If they don't satisfy you, nothing will, and I shall have to take her to another manager.'

" ' Show me the certificates ! ' said I.

" Well ! he produced them on the spot, and they seemed all right. Of course I couldn't read a word of them, but they had a lot of sealing-wax on them, which is always convincing, and had a genuine official look. I wanted the girl so bad that, perhaps, it led me to be a little careless for once in my life ; so I said to the agent that I would give him twenty-five dollars a week, and sign a contract with him for a year. We argued the matter for about an hour, and finally we came to an agreement on the basis of seventy-five dollars a week and three benefits a year. It was the steepest price I ever paid, but I was losing money at the rate of fifty dollars a week, and I was ready to take almost any chance of bringing up the business again. Besides, I knew that if the Two-Headed Girl didn't draw I should be ruined anyhow, and it didn't matter what I might agree to pay, as there would be no money to pay it with. Whereas if she did draw, as I expected she would, I could easy afford to pay seventy-five dollars a week for her. I always did go on the principle of dealing liberally with people, especially when it is clear that there is nothing to be lost by it.

"While the agent and I were trying to get the best of one another the Two-Headed Girl sat with some of her arms around both her necks, and was that patient and sweet-tempered in appearance that I began to hope that for once I had found a ' freak ' that wouldn't be perpetually quarrelling. As I have told you, I presume, ' freaks ' do nothing but quarrel and fall in love. I don't wonder at their quarrelling, seeing that they are shut up together day and night, and haven't anything else to do; but it was a long time before I found out why they are constantly falling in love. It is because they don't get any exercise, except now and then a drive in a closed carriage.

"You never hear of a trapeze performer or a Strong Man falling in love; that's because they work off their affections on their muscles. On the other hand, a Fat Woman, who never gets any exercise at all, is always in love, and generally two or three deep. Naturally, the more ' freaks ' fall in love the more they quarrel, and there is hardly a day that I don't have to smooth two or three of them down, or threaten to lock them up till they quit heaving candlesticks and language at one another.

"Well, I advertised my Two-Headed Girl the next day, and when night came the house was packed. Ralph Waldo Emerson himself couldn't have drawn

"THE VERY BEST CLASSES OF BOSTON SOCIETY."

better. The very best classes of Boston society came to see the Two-Headed Girl, and more women with more spectacles and more false teeth came into the show than I had ever seen before in my whole

professional experience.   The men and women used
to stand by the hour in front of the sofa where the
Two-Headed Girl sat and argue about her soul,
which, considering that her soul wasn't on exhibition, seemed to me a loss of time.   They made out
in some way that I don't pretend to understand, that
the Girl had something to do with philosophy, and
that her two heads proved something or other that
Mr. Emerson used to teach.

"You've heard of Mr. Emerson, of course.   He
was what they called a philosopher, and drew better
than any ' freak ' or primer donner that ever visited
Boston.   I couldn't see anything in him, myself.
I went to hear him lecture once, and it seemed to
me that he wasn't to be compared with Artemus
Ward.   However, that was none of my business,
though at one time I did think of making him a
handsome offer to join my combination.

"There wasn't the least doubt about the success
of the Two-Headed Girl.   In the very first week I
took in two hundred and thirty dollars more than I
had ever taken in any one week in my life before.
The museum was crowded day and night, and every
mother in Boston brought her children and told
them that the Two-Headed Girl taught some great
moral lesson, and that they ought to imitate her, or

"I DON'T ALLOW NO QUARRELLING."

avoid imitating her, or some other rubbish of that
general kind. I never pretend to understand such
things myself. I don't associate with 'freaks' to
learn moral lessons from them. When I want
moral lessons I'll go to Sunday-school and get 'em,
instead of lowering myself to ask 'freaks' to give
me lessons.

" The Two-Headed Girl, as I have said in the beginning, was a Laplander, and couldn't speak anything but Laplandish. She had been with me
about a month when I was astonished, one night
after the exhibition had closed, and the 'freaks' had
sat down to their usual banquet of pickles and cider,
to hear one of her heads say to the other :—

" ' You say that again, miss, and I'll tear your
eyes out ! '

" ' Halloa ! ' says I, ' thought neither of you could
speak any English ? '

" ' The Girl blushed a double blush on all four
cheeks, and said, ' We've learned considerable since
we came to America,. but we never try to speak
English because it ain't professional—not in our
case, at any rate.'

" ' That's all right,' said I. ' Speak what you
like, only remember that I don't allow no quarrelling among my people.'

5

" The next day I made inquiries about the Two-Headed Girl, and found out that both of her were in love with the same young man. He came to the show every day and always brought both of her

" HE ALWAYS BROUGHT BOTH OF HER FLOWERS."

flowers. I found out afterwards that he was a philosopher, and was studying what he called 'The Psychological Character of Female Dual Consciousness as Exemplified in the Two-Headed Girl of Lapland'. I remember this because he wrote an article in the *Atlantic Monthly* with that title, which would have been a first-class advertisement of the Girl if she hadn't happened to have retired to private life when the article was published. He was a rather good-looking young fellow, and both the heads of the Girl considered that he was in love with them. Mary, which is what we used to call the right-hand head, was sure that the young man was after her, and only gave flowers to Jane, who was the left-hand head, in order not to give away the real state of his affections to the general public; while Jane was equally certain that it was she the young man was in love with, and that he considered the other head to be very much in the way.

"The Fat Woman, who sat close to the Two-Headed Girl on the stage, was really frightened at the way the two heads used to go on. She could hear them whispering to each other when the audience couldn't hear anything said. Mary would put her cheek up against Jane's and smile so sweetly that the audience would say: 'How perfectly lovely!' but all the time she would be saying: 'I'd like to bite your ugly ear off, miss!' and then presently Jane would put her arm around Mary's neck and whisper: 'You mean, deceitful

thing! Wait till we get to our room, and I'll let
you know!' The Fat Woman, who was all the
time reading Dime novels, said she was afraid
some awful tragedy was preparing, and that
presently the place would be drowned in blood.
She wasn't altogether wrong, as you'll see presently.

"One night, just after the banquet was over,
and the 'freaks' had mostly gone to their rooms,
we heard such a dismal shrieking from the Two-
Headed Girl's room that we all rushed to the door.
That is, when I say 'all,' I mean the Giant and
the Living Skeleton, who had been sitting up with
me a little later than usual. I never allow nothing
improper on the part of nobody in my show, and
I set the example in such matters myself. So I
told the Giant and the Skeleton that we would
withdraw, while the Strong Woman would burst
the door open and see what was the matter.

"Accordingly we did so, and the Strong Woman
set her shoulder against the door, and it just sort
of melted away, as you might say. She told me
that she found the Two-Headed Girl having the
liveliest kind of a fight with herself. She was lying
on the floor, and the half of her which was upper-
most, and which happened to be Mary, was laying
into the other half and hauling out the hair and

the hairpins by handfuls. The Strong Woman, wanting to check the effusion of hair, went to work to separate them, and succeeded altogether too

"THE STRONG WOMAN SET HER SHOULDER AGAINST THE DOOR."

well. In fact, when she got hold of Mary, and tried to pull her clear of Jane's hair, the two girls came apart altogether. The Strong Woman, who like the rest of us had believed in the Two-Headed

Girl, was that frightened when she saw that she
had pulled her clean apart that she in turn yelled
for help.

"This time I had to lay aside my scruples and
see for myself what was the matter. There sat the
Strong Woman on the floor, holding half of the
Two-Headed Girl in her arms, and there lay the
other half, two or three yards off, on the carpet,
crying her level best, and cussin' the rest of her in
language which, if I am any judge of language,
and I ought to be, was learned somewhere down by
the wharves. When I saw that Jane was more
frightened than hurt, I told her to go to bed, and
told the Strong Woman to take Mary into her
room for the night. Mary went peaceably, for
when the Strong Woman got hold of anybody, male
or female, they generally did as she said.

"The next day I called up the Two-Headed
Girl and told them that our contract was at an end.
'I will never,' I said, 'be a party to a fraud on the
public, especially when it is sure to be found out,
as this fraud of yours is. A committee of Boston
surgeons was going to examine you this very day,
and I, believing you to be genuine, was to offer
them every facility. What I am offering now is a
free passage for you both, from here to New York,

and don't you ever let me hear of your trying to exhibit again, or I'll come out and tell the truth about you.'

" That was my only attempt at exhibiting a Two-Headed Girl. I ought not to be hard on the girls, for they pulled me through a very tight place in my professional career; but at the same time they took me in, and not being a part of the public I don't like to be took in. However, it all happened long ago, and I defy any ' freak' to play any sort of game on me again. If there is any deceit to be practised in my show, I conceive that I am the one to do it, and not the one to be practised on."

CHAPTER V.

HOW THE FAT WOMAN ELOPED.

"YES, sir," continued the door-keeper; "Fat Women are more sentimental than any other women. The fatter they are the more they fall in love. Though, to tell the truth, the most sentimental Fat Woman I ever had wasn't by any means the fattest. She only weighed two hundred and eighty pounds when she came to me, and I lost her when she had just got up to three hundred and forty; and very sorry I was to lose her, for she had a great future before her if she had only been

(6₄)

willing to stick to business and had kept up her pride in her profession.

"For the first six months I had her I thought she was a jewel. She never took the least bit of exercise, and she dieted as carefully as if she had been a dyspeptic with a stomach in ruins, who was trying to put himself to rights again by eating nothing but the most disagreeable kinds of food. By the way, did you ever notice that the only way to get even with a stomach that has once gone back on you is to starve it, or give it nothing that any rational stomach likes? The minute you begin to treat a stomach kindly, and let it have the sort of meat and drink it wants, that minute you are on the road to dyspepsia. A stomach is just like a small boy—you'll spoil it if you ever let it have its own way.

"I hadn't had this Fat Woman a week when I saw that she was as bad as all the rest of them, so far as falling in love goes. Our Giant was taken with the scarlet fever, which was a most ridiculous sort of disease for a man of six feet and a half high, and mighty sick he was. Of course, I couldn't send him to a hospital, where everybody could see him, without destroying his market value, so he had to be nursed in his room at the Museum.

Nobody was willing to nurse him till the Fat Woman came forward and said that she would nurse the poor man if everybody else was afraid. Naturally, everybody applauded her bravery, as everybody always does when a person undertakes to do something that other people are afraid to do, and are glad to get rid of doing. I didn't altogether like the idea of temporarily losing the services of the Fat Woman as well as the Giant, but I like to let my people have all the pleasure they can, so I told the Fat Woman to go ahead, and I would pay her half her salary while she was off duty.

"Of course, the Fat Woman fell in love with the Giant before she had been twenty-four hours in the sick room, but I will say that she made a first-class nurse. There was no walking around the room, and knocking over bottles, and putting the furniture in order, and sweeping the floor up, as is always going on when you have an ordinary-sized nurse. The Fat Woman spent the whole day and night sitting in her chair, except when the Giant wanted his medicine, or when he tried to get up, being delirious, and go on the platform in his nightshirt. Whenever this fit was on him, the Fat Woman would just lean her weight on him till he quieted down.

" Once she accidentally leaned a little too much on his chest, and the man was pretty nearly suffocated before she noticed that anything unusual was the matter, but generally speaking she did her duty in a way that laid over any regular hospital nurse that I ever saw.

" When the Giant got well the Fat Woman, who considered herself engaged to him, though he swore that he had never said a word of the kind, expected him to marry her, and when she found out that he hadn't the least idea of any such foolishness she was destroyed, as you might say. For about a week she lost her appetite and didn't eat enough to keep her alive, not to speak of making progress in her profession, and I had to speak pretty sharply to her about the dishonesty of growing thin when she had a contract with me that obliged her to increase her weight by all legitimate means. However, at the end of the week she braced up again and soon got over her passion.

" That's the way with Fat Women. They get over their disappointments, and are looking out for fresh ones quicker than any other women outside of a Dime Museum. I'd like to find some intelligent man, say a parson or a doctor, who could tell me the reason of this. I can't see myself why there

should be any difference between a fat woman and
a thin woman in the matter of their affections; but
there is a big difference.   If you want just to carry
on with a girl, take a middling fat one, and she'll
get over it without giving you any trouble.   But if
you mean business, and want to marry a girl who'll
stick to you, don't you take any girl weighing more
than a hundred and twenty pounds.

"In course of time the Fat Woman forgot all
about her affair with the Giant, and the two were
excellent friends, both being good-tempered and
good-hearted in their way.   But pretty soon the Fat
Woman fell in love again, and this time it was with
an outsider.   He was a sort of ticket speculator, and
about as worthless a fellow as there was in all Cincinnati, which was where my show was located at
the time, and anybody except a Fat Woman would
have known that if he made love to a woman it was
because he thought there was money in it.   He supposed that the Fat Woman was well-to-do in the
world, as most of them are, seeing as they draw
good salaries and have no expenses to speak of.
Besides, he was sharp enough to see that she was
putting on flesh day by day, and would naturally
command more and more salary according as her
weight increased.   He used to come into my place

pretty nearly every day and have a little talk with
the Fat Woman, and say how-de-do to the other

"THE TWO WERE EXCELLENT FRIENDS."

'freaks,' and maybe try to borrow fifty cents of me,
for I had known him a good many years—which

naturally made him feel that he had a right to borrow money of me.

"One day I noticed that the Fat Woman looked a good deal smaller round the waist than usual, and I charged her with lacing. At first she denied it, but I told her it was no use, and that she couldn't deceive me, and then she admitted that she was wearing a corset. 'What's got into you?' I asked her. 'Haven't you no sense, and no pride in your profession? Here you are actually trying to make yourself look smaller than you are, when you know perfectly well that you ought to be trying to do just the opposite. I tell you what it is, Melinda, you've got your eye on some young man, and want to make yourself look pretty.'

"'And what if I do?' said she. 'Do you think that a Fat Woman hasn't got any feelings? I'm a woman, if I do weigh three hundred pounds, and I've got a woman's feelings, though none of you men ever seem to think so.' I told her that there wasn't any question about her feelings, and that I had no concern with anything but her weight, and that if she began to lose flesh she couldn't expect me to stick to the contract. 'Just put all this foolishness out of your mind,' I said, 'and try to work yourself up to four hundred pounds. That's an

ambition worthy of a sensible woman, while thishyer falling in love is only fit for women who haven't
got brains or flesh to earn their own living.'

"But my advice was wasted, as advice always is,
and in a few days the Fat Woman came to me and
asked to be let off her contract, so that she could
be married and go to keeping house for her husband.
It made me mad to see her so willing to throw
away her future, and so careless about my own
interests, considering that I had treated her kindly
and liberally, and I told her that I should hold her
to her contract, which had two years more to run,
and would sue her for damages if she left me, or if
she neglected to keep herself up to her usual weight.
This made her pretty angry, and she said that she
should do as she pleased, and that I was a horrid
brute. So I saw that I was going to have trouble
with her.

"That night the Fat Woman had a long talk
with her admirer after the performance was over,
and for the next day or two was in such good spirits
that I knew she must mean mischief. The fact
was that the fellow had induced her to agree to
elope with him, and she felt so sure that her professional career was coming to a happy end that
she openly took to drinking vinegar and eating

meat, and drew in her waist till she looked as if she was on the edge of apoplexy.

"I LOOKED OUT OF THE WINDOW."

"The Fat Woman's room was just over mine, and naturally she couldn't move round much without waking me, though I am a pretty middling sound sleeper. Soon after she had taken to vinegar, I was waked up one night by hearing her walking about her room in her boots, and as my watch said it was two o'clock, I knew something was up. By-and-by she came downstairs as softly as she could, though the stairs did groan as stairs will when you put three hundred pounds of woman on them in the middle of the night. I got up and looked out of the window, and there was a carriage standing by the stage door. I saw the Fat Woman's little game at once. She was going to run away with the ticket speculator.

" My first thought was to dress and run out and stop her, but presently I remembered how narrow the stage door was, and I made up my mind to wait and see the fun : my window being where it commanded a good view of the scene of action. Just as I anticipated, the Fat Woman halted when she came to the stage door, and presently I heard her call in a low voice : ' Tom, come and help me, I'm stuck in the door!' Tom climbed down out of the carriage, and getting a good hold of one of the Fat Woman's arms, braced himself against the jamb of the door and pulled his level best. But he couldn't start her, and though she stood it like a heroine, she had to tell him, after he had

6

pulled a while, that she couldn't stand it any longer.

"Then Tom tried to push her back into the corridor, so that she could take a fresh start and maybe get herself through the door edgewise, but

"HE PULLED HIS LEVEL BEST."

he couldn't budge her. So the two whispered together a while, and then Tom called the driver of the carriage to come and help him. The driver was the most intelligent of the lot, and he said that the only way to get the lady loose was for Tom to climb over her and then push from the inside while the driver pulled from the outside. It didn't seem to be an easy job for Tom to climb over her, but he managed to do it, though she screamed a little when his boots sunk into her shoulders. Then I heard him say: 'Now, driver, while you pull I'll try running the length of the corridor and bumping her. The shock may loosen her if you pull just as I bump.' I don't know how the Fat Woman liked it, but she held her tongue, and after a while something gave way, and she suddenly shot out into the road, falling on the driver, and making him think his last end had come. When he got himself free, and he and Tom together had set the Fat Woman on her legs again, I heard him say: 'I'll have to be after charging you, sor, for a suit of clothes, being as my own is spoilt entirely, and my left arm is sprained'. But Tom told him to hurry up and help boost the Fat Woman into the carriage, and he'd see that everything was made right when the time came to pay.

"You may ask why I didn't interfere about this time, and keep the woman from running away. Because I knew just what her weight was, and how much the bottom of an ordinary carriage will bear, and I wanted to see how the thing would end.

"Well, it ended just as I knew it would. It was

the middle of summer, and daylight began about three o'clock, so Tom was in a hurry to get away before anybody would see him and recognise him or his companion. He and the driver gave the Fat Woman a most everlasting boost and shot her into the carriage, and Tom was going to get in after her when I heard something crack, and the Fat Woman gave a dismal yell. She had gone clean through the bottom of the carriage, and was standing with her feet on the road, with the broken pieces of the flooring holding her so tight that she couldn't stir. She gave up all pretence of keeping quiet, and called out at the top of her voice for the driver to hold the horses and keep the carriage from moving ; and she begged Tom, if he had any love for her, to help her out of the carriage, and let her get into her own room once more.

" The fact is, the woman was in a very bad fix. The splinters must have hurt her like so many knives, and the more Tom tried to pull away the broken boards, the more they got their work in. Then all of a sudden the horses took it into their heads to start, and the woman yelled that they were killing her, and the driver must cut them loose instantly.

" By the time the horses were unhitched Tom had given up the attempt to get the woman loose as a

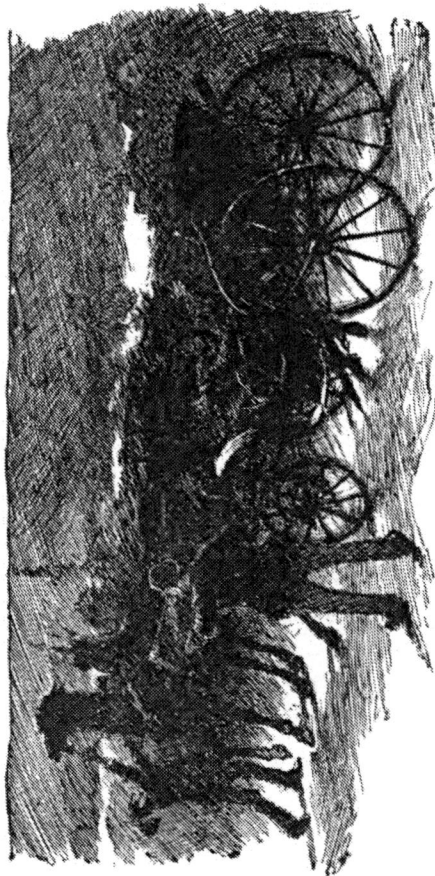

"THE WOMAN YELLED THAT THEY WERE KILLING HER."

bad job, and was standing in a helpless sort of way
by the carriage door, telling her for Heaven's sake
to hold her tongue before she waked up the whole
neighbourhood.

"I judged it was about time for me to take a hand
in the proceedings, so I called out of the window:
'Melinda! If you've had enough of thishyer foolishness, just say the word, and I'll come down with an
axe and help you out of your fix.' She said all she
wanted was to be let loose, and she would never try
to leave me again, not for any man, let alone a cruel,
heartless wretch that would stand by and see a
woman suffer, and never lift a finger to help her.
So I dressed slow and easy, so as to let the splinters
sink into her mind as you might say, and keep her
from forgetting all she owed me, and then I got my
axe and came down and broke her out without much
trouble. Tom had nothing to say for himself. I
will give him the credit of admitting that he stood
around while I was working with the axe, till he saw
that the woman was loose, and then he bolted, thinking, perhaps, that I might be disposed to use the
axe on him, which would have been a waste of
labour that I shouldn't have thought of undertaking.
The driver tackled up his horses in no time and
started after Tom as hard as he could drive, know-

ing that his chance of collecting payment would be middling small if he let Tom fairly out of his sight.

"The Fat Woman was a good deal tore up with

the splinters, and more or less exhausted by the mental strain she had gone through while the two men were trying to haul her through the stage door. She hadn't much strength left for conversation, and she went very quietly with me round to the front of the house and through the big door up to her room. When she was going into her room she turned and said :—

"'Colonel, I'll never do it again, and I'll do my best to fatten up after this '.

"'That's all right,' said I.   'You just go to bed again and forget all about it.   We're all liable to make mistakes, and it wasn't your fault that you didn't know how much a floor of a carriage would bear.   I'll send you up the arnica, and just you use it and forget all about Tom, who is no good anyway, and who'll never come round you again, you can bet your bottom dollar.'

"After that you never saw a more faithful and conscientious artist than that Fat Woman.   She dieted herself more carefully than ever, and before the year was out she had got up to three hundred and forty pounds."

CHAPTER VI.

THE N'SHUGIE-GUMBO.

"FROM what you have told me," I said to the door-keeper, "I gather that 'freaks,' as a rule, are not overburdened with brains."

"There ain't brains enough in an ordinary Dime Museum, all put together, to fit out even a member of Congress. Why, if you could take the brains of all my company, barring the Dwarf's, and put them in the skull of a second-rate temperance orator, you'd find that they'd rattle round like dried peas. You see 'freaks' make their living by careful cultivation of their bodies. Naturally, their minds are no sort of use to them. What's the good of a mind to a Fat Woman ? What she requires to succeed in her profession is flesh, not intellect. It's the same way with all the rest of them, excepting the Lightning Calculator, and even he needs 'cheek' more than he does mind.

" Of course," continued the door-keeper, " there's exceptions to every rule. Now, my Dwarf is as bright a chap as you can find in any newspaper office in the country, and it is ˙my experience that the smartest class of men we have are the newspaper reporters. I never try to fool a reporter. If I see one coming into my show I just open a bottle of wine for him, and I say : ' You'll see that the Gorilla, or maybe the Fat Woman, isn't quite according to the small bills ; but strange coincidences will happen in this world, and if you shouldn't give me away, and if you should receive a ten-dollar bill in an anonymous letter the next day, it would be a coincidence that would be pleasant as well as im-

proving for all concerned'. I never yet had a reporter prove himself unworthy of my confidence.
They are a high-minded, honourable class, provided you pay up handsomely, and never deceive
them.

"But I was going to tell you about my Dwarf.
He is about forty years old, as I should judge, and
he has spent the best part of his life in inventing
things. Some of his inventions are useful ones,
and he holds two or three patents that have involved
him in a lot of lawsuits and cost him no end of
money, which, as everybody knows, is what a
successful invention always does. He was working
at one time on a patent umbrella gun and shield,
which he expected would be adopted by every army
in the world, and would make him a millionaire
half a dozen times over. His first idea was to
make a combined umbrella and sword-cane. He
made an umbrella with a stout handle, and fitted
the handle with a sword, which, when it was thrown
out by a spring, projected about two feet from the
end of the stick.

"Well! he saw after a while that the only way
this weapon could be used was by treating it like a
gun with a fixed bayonet, so he modified his sword
by turning it into a regular sword bayonet. Then

it occurred to him that if he turned the umbrella stick into a rifle he would have a better weapon

"USEFUL FOR KEEPING OFF THE RAIN."

still, so he substituted a Remington rifle for his umbrella stick, and fitted an ordinary umbrella

frame to it. What he really had at this stage of the proceedings was a rifle with an umbrella attachment. It was useful for keeping off the rain, provided any one wanted to carry such a heavy weight; but, as I told him one day when he was showing the model to me, most people would prefer an umbrella weighing less than sixteen pounds.

" The next thing he did with that invention was to make his umbrella shot-proof. This was, according to him, the biggest invention since the invention of fire-arms. His idea was that a regiment of soldiers armed with his umbrella could advance on the enemy, firing as they advanced, and sheltering themselves behind their umbrellas so that it wouldn't be possible for them to get hit, except, perhaps, in the lower part of the leg. He was so sure that he had made the greatest invention of the age that he got pretty angry with me when I asked him what material he calculated to make his umbrella out of. ' Steel,' said he. ' Thin steel; just thick enough to resist a rifle bullet.' ' And how are you going to shut your steel umbrella when it ain't in use ? ' says I. ' Colonel ! ' says he, very dignified, and mad enough to try his rifle on me, ' if you'll attend to your part of thishyer show, I'll attend to mine.'

" Well, that Dwarf worked at that invention for

more than a year. He managed to make a steel
umbrella that
would shut up
after a fashion,
but it weighed
about a hun-
dred pounds.
Then he tried
making his um-
brella of steel
chain-work, like
the sort of old
armour those
chaps in the
Crusades used
to wear, but it
weighed almost
as much as the
solid steel, and
then it let in
water like a
sieve, and was
of no sort of use
as an umbrella
against the rain.

" COMPLETE."

"Of course, this didn't suit him, so he covered

his chain-armour with rubber-cloth and made a small hole in it near the top with a trap door to open and shut, so as a soldier could take aim through it when the umbrella was open. But he wasn't satisfied yet, and that invention kept on growing. The Dwarf made an extension of canvas to button on to the sides of the umbrella, so as to make a tent of the whole affair. All you had to do was to button on this extension, and then dig a hole in the ground for the butt of the gun. When you had planted the gun in this hole, and opened the umbrella and pegged it down all round, you had a first-class circular tent.

"By this time the thing had got to weigh so much that no man could have carried it on a march, but the Dwarf fitted a wheel on to the muzzle of the gun, so that the thing could be wheeled like a wheelbarrow. When he had put hooks on to the under side of the gun for a knapsack and a haversack, and a cartridge box, and a blanket, and all the rest of a man's kit, he considered that the invention was about complete. But he couldn't get the Government or anybody else to do anything but laugh at it, so he finally gave it up as a bad job, and worked off his steel umbrella frames on the Fat Woman as the latest style of crinoline. But all this goes to

show that the Dwarf was a person with intellects
into him. I can't say much for his morals, or his
temper, but there is no doubt that he did have
brains.

" He came to me one day about two years ago and
said: ' Colonel, I understand that all your monkeys
are dead '. You see, I had taken a cage of six monkeys
from a friend of mine, who was in the menagerie line,
in payment of a bad debt, and the monkeys had
proved a strong attraction while they lasted. However, the climate finished them after a while, as it
always will do, and all that was left of them was the
big empty cage.

" ' You know well enough the monkeys are dead,'
says I to the Dwarf.   ' But what's that to you ?
They weren't any relations of yours, so far as I
know.'

" ' How would you like a first-class trained orang-
outang ? ' says the Dwarf.   ' One that could smoke,
and let on to read a newspaper, and do all them sort
of tricks ? '

" ' Are you thinking of applying for the place ? '
I asked, not feeling in particularly good temper myself that morning, for something, I forget what, had
gone wrong with me.

" ' Just so,' says he.   ' I've studied up the monkey

7

business since you had those monkeys here, and I
can do it as well as the best of them. Come along
to the cage and I'll show you something.'

"I went along with him, and when we got to the
cage the Dwarf pulls off his shoes and stockings,
and jumps up against the side of the cage, clutching
the bars with his hands and feet at the same time
just as a monkey would do. Then he chatters, and
makes a grab for my watch chain, and would
have got it, too, if I hadn't jumped back pretty
spry.

"'How do I do it?' asked the Dwarf.

"'Better than the other monkeys,' said I.

"'Well!' says he. 'I'm ready to be an orang-
outang in the afternoon and a Dwarf at night, if
you'll double my salary. That is, as soon as I get
my tail perfected.'

"'What are you giving us?' said I. 'Orang-
outangs don't have no tails.'

"'This here one does,' said the Dwarf, 'and it's
going to be a practicable tail too. I have been working at it for the last week, and I shall have it after
a bit in such a state that I can hook it around a
chandelier and swing head downwards. That will
convince the public that I am genuine. It's easy
to dress up like any animal, except an elephant, or

maybe a camelopard, but it's the tail that always
gives a man away. And if you don't have a tail,

" DISCOVERED BY STANLEY."

people will think that you shirked it because you
knew you were playing a game on them, and couldn't
succeed if you put on a tail. Now, my tail will be

the very thing that will convince the public that
they are looking at a real orang-outang, and not at
a Chinaman, like your last Gorilla.'

"'You might be a new sort of monkey discovered
by Stanley in Central Africa, and sent over to me
as a special testimonial of friendship,' says I, for I
was beginning to think that the little man's idea was
a good one. 'You get up a practicable tail, and a
good general disguise, and I'll agree to your terms
and maybe do something better still.' So it was
agreed that as soon as the Dwarf could invent a
satisfactory tail, he should be brought out as a
learned ape.

"That tail was one of the best things the Dwarf
ever invented. It was made of steel, with no end
of joints, and was about as flexible as the real article.
It was contrived so that whenever the Dwarf took a
turn with it around anything, it would keep its hold
till he released it by touching a spring somewhere
about his waist. His general make-up was superb.
He wasn't content with just putting on a skin, and
painting his face a little, but he padded himself here
and there, and wore a flexible mask that was twice
as ugly and just as probable as any monkey's face
you ever saw. When he first showed himself to me
in this get-up I saw at once that he was going to be

a big success, and when he hooked his tail over the
Strong Woman's horizontal bar, and swung head

"HE SWUNG HEAD DOWNWARDS."

downwards, and chattered and cussed in the monkey
dialect, there wasn't a scientific chap in all Chicago,

to say nothing of a regular menagerie sharp, who could have supposed that he wasn't genuine.

"What with drawing two salaries, and having a fair opportunity to play tricks on the public, the Dwarf was a middling happy man. There was always a crowd round his cage, and nobody seemed to read the notices warning people not to go within reach of the N'Shugie-Gumbo, which was the name a friend of mine, who had read a lot about Central Africa, gave him. The Dwarf would sit and look at the people in the solemnest kind of way for a few minutes, and then he would come to the front of the cage and put his arm through the bars to shake hands.

"Everybody would want to shake hands with him, and presently he would get a chance to snatch a woman's bonnet. He would haul it through the bars, and then he would hook his tail over a horizontal bar that was in the cage, and swing comfortably while he pulled the bonnet into shreds. Of course, the woman would yell, but everybody else would be delighted, and the Dwarf, having a natural love for malicious mischief, would be as happy as they make 'em. Then he would lay for spectacles, and if any man or woman wearing glasses came inside his reach, he would snatch their glasses and break them into bits before they could fairly realise what was the matter.

" Occasionally when a man lost a pair of gold spectacles, he would appeal to me, and I would go into the cage with a whip, and make the monkey disgorge, which he always did after making sure that he had bent them up about as far as they could be bent.

" Then, in addition to his fun, the Dwarf had lots of candy and apples and such given to him, and what he didn't eat on the spot he used to hide under a blanket in the corner till the show was over. As for cigars, he used to get the best part of a box every day. The people were just wild to see him smoke, and they said he did it just like a human be-ing. He used to smoke pretty near the whole after-noon, and when the show closed he would have a double handful of cigars to carry to his room. All the other ' freaks' were raging with envy at his good luck, and being, as I said, naturally vicious, this only made him the happier. Nobody outside of my establishment had the least idea that the N'Shugie-Gumbo wasn't a genuine Central African monkey, and a scientific chap belonging to the Chicago University wrote a paper about him to show that he was a missing lynx, which to my mind

showed how big an idiot a scientific chap can be,
for the Dwarf wasn't missing, and he wasn't the
least bit like a lynx.

"JUST LIKE A HUMAN BEING."

"He was climbing into his cage one afternoon,
just before the show opened, and as I was passing
by I asked him how things were going with him.

"'I don't feel easy about that tail,' says he. 'It

don't work altogether right. Yesterday, when I had
it hooked round the bar I couldn't get it loose again
for about half an hour, and was afraid I should have
to call for help, which would have been the ruin
of me. I've examined it, and I can't find anything
the matter with it. I suppose it's just the cussedness
of the spring, that'll work sometimes, and sometimes
it won't. I'm a little afraid that it'll get me into a
scrape yet before this thing is played out.'

" I remembered these remarks afterwards, for they
seemed to be sort of prophetic, as you might say.
That very afternoon the tail failed to do its work,
and the Dwarf's experience as a monkey had to be
brought to a close. My own idea is that the tail
needed to be oiled, or else that the spring had got
bent in some way. Anyway, it got the Dwarf into
the worst trouble that he ever got into while he was
with me.

" It happened in the course of the afternoon, when
the house was pretty full, and there was a big crowd
round the monkey's cage, that the Dwarf accidentally let his tail slip through the bars and hang
down where the people could reach it. There was
a woman standing close to the cage, and she thought
it would be smart to take hold of the end of the tail
and give it a pull. Accordingly, she did so, and the

minute she took the tail in her hand, it curled round
her wrist, and there she was, held fast.   As I told
you, the tail acted automatically, and whatever it
took hold of it held on to till the Dwarf touched the
spring that released it.

"IT CURLED ROUND HER WRIST."

"Of course, as soon as the Dwarf saw what was
up, he tried to let go his hold of the woman's hand,
but the spring wouldn't work, and the woman began
to get frightened, and cried for help.   Two or three
men came to her assistance, and tried their level
best to untwist the tail, but it was made of the best

steel, and they couldn't do anything with it. Then, seeing that the woman was half-frightened to death, a man pulled out a knife and started in to cut the monkey's tail off. He hadn't more than turned the edge of his knife on the steel, and cut his own fingers, when another man—a big fellow, who had something to do with the Society for Prevention of Cruelty— fetched him one under the ear that laid him out, re- marking as he did so, in a quiet way, that there wasn't going to be no cruelty to no animals while he was on hand.

"All this time the Dwarf was fumbling away, trying to make the spring work, and so get his tail loose before anything serious should happen. It wasn't long before it did happen. The big man who was opposed to cruelty to animals said that all that was needed to make the monkey listen to reason was firmness and gentleness, and that if any one would pull steadily on the tail the monkey would be glad to let the woman loose. Accordingly he laid hold of the tail, and two or three other chaps laid hold of it too, just to show how anxious they were to help the poor woman. A gentle pull didn't have any effect on the monkey except to haul him tight up against the bars, and the man who had been knocked down for trying to use his knife began to relieve his feelings by getting the big man by the collar, and trying to pull him backwards. What with hanging on to the tail so as to keep himself on his feet, and what with being a little excited, the big man pulled harder than he meant to, and the men that were helping him pulled their heaviest.

"The long and short of it was that the tail, which had never been built to stand such a strain, gave way, and most of the public that were standing close to the cage went down on the floor in a heap.

"When the big man got up, waving the tail in the air, with its leather fastenings and buckles and such in plain sight, the Dwarf knew that it was all up with the N'Shugie-Gumbo. In similar circumstances an audience generally cleans out the establishment, and that is what would probably have happened on this occasion, if it hadn't been that a free fight was going on among the men that had been knocked over when the tail gave way, and they had no time to attend to serious things. I called in a couple of policemen and had the whole lot arrested for breach of the peace, and it being by that time about the hour for closing, I induced everybody to leave by offering them their money back. You can bet I felt relieved when the last man had gone, for if the crowd had undertook to clean out the place they would have killed the Dwarf for certain.

"'I don't so much mind giving up the monkey business,' said the Dwarf to me that evening, 'for I was beginning to get tired of it; but I do hate to quit without ever having got hold of a wig. I've had more than thirty bonnets, and fifteen spectacles, but I've never been able to grab any man's wig, though I've come near it two or three times. Well, I suppose we can't have everything here to please us. I've had a good time while it lasted, and I suppose I ought to be satisfied. But I should like to have stole just one wig.'

" He was the most intelligent 'freak' I ever knew, and that steel tail of his was a mighty smart invention; but I told him that, after considering all things, I should expect him to stick to the legitimate, and should refuse to give my sanction to any more plans for deluding the public, seeing as they are nearly always failures in the long run."

CHAPTER VII.

THE MERMAID.

" WHAT I need," said the door-keeper one evening,
when he had seemed more than usually thoughtful,
" is some brand new attraction. Thishyer thing of
running the same show year after year, with the
same Giant and Dwarf and Fat Woman and such,

doesn't seem worthy of an enterprising Christian man. "

" I thought you had tried novel attractions a good many times ? " said I.

" So I have, but they never panned out well. I told you about several of them, and you could see for yourself that they were failures. You've got to deal honestly with the public if you want to succeed. Of course, when I say honestly I mean it in a reasonable sort of way. If you take your honesty straight, it won't work. You've got to mix it with a little intelligent enterprise before it can really be called the best policy.

" One of the best things that I ever tried in the line of novel attractions," continued the door-keeper, after a smoky pause, " was the Marquesas Mermaid. She drew full houses day and night all the time I had her, which was about six weeks. I judged that she was worth to me all of two hundred and fifty dollars a week above her expenses while she lasted, but I had to pay her in damages more than she ever brought me. Probably it served me right for deceiving the public more than the public ought to be deceived, but that isn't any consolation to me. I'm willing to stand the loss of a fair amount of money, and I don't mind being pitched into, to a moderate

extent, by my conscience; but to lose your money
and to have your conscience pegging away at you at
the same time is a little too much, and that's what
happened to me in this Mermaid affair.

" She was brought to me by a stranger one day.
I knew him by reputation, and his reputation was
pretty bad, but I had never dealt with him before.
I was exhibiting in New York at the time, and was
doing a fair to middling business, though it showed
signs of falling off, owing to the Presidential cam-
paign which was then in progress.   If ever you go
into the show business you'll wish you were living
under a king.   Thishyer electing of a President takes
the public's attention away from all freaks excepting political ones, and people will walk ten miles
to look at Jim Blaine sooner than walk around the
corner to see a first-class Fat Woman.   I believed
in a republic as much as anybody before I went into
the show business, but there is no denying the fact
that no Museum of Freaks can stand the active
competition of American politics.

" Well! to go back to thishyer Mermaid.   I was
sitting in my office one day when this agent comes
to me and says :—

" ' Colonel ! if you want an attraction that will
knock all competition sky-high, including the Eye-

talian Opera and the Woman's Temperance Society, I've got it for you.'

" 'What is it?' said I. 'Not that I'm in need of any attraction, considering that I'm turning about a thousand people away every day; but for all that, I'm always ready to consider any fair offer. That is, providing it ain't no Two-Headed Girl. One head apiece is all any freak that gets into my collection is allowed to have.'

" You see," added the door-keeper, " I'd been sold once, and put in a very bad position, by a Two-Headed Girl, and I wasn't going to be caught in that way a second time.

" ' It's a genuwine South Sea Mermaid,' said the agent, ' and a mighty handsome one too.'

" ' Then we can't trade,' said I. ' I've got one of your South Sea Mermaids in one of my packing boxes, and I'll give her to you if you'll carry her away. A Mermaid won't draw now-a-days any more than a stuffed cat.'

" ' But,' says the man, ' this is none of your regular old-style Mermaids, made out of a fish and a monkey. I tell you she's a genuwine Mermaid, what sings and swims, and combs her hair, and talks. Mighty intelligent she is, too. She can speak French just as well as you or me speaks American, though, of

8

course, she don't speak it in public.   If you'll let
me bring her here some morning and give you a
private exhibition, you'll admit that she is something altogether new in the Mermaid line.'

"The next morning, when there was nobody in
the Museum except me, a van drove up, and a big
packing box mounted on wheels was brought in.
The agent was with it, and when he had sent away
the men that brought the box, he opened it.   There
was a big glass tank inside of it, and inside of the
tank was a very handsome young woman, got up as
a Mermaid.   And she was mighty well got up, too.
The upper part of her was covered with india-rubber
life preservers fitted to her shape, and from the waist
down she was covered with a blue and gold fish skin
that ended in a practicable tail worked by her feet.
What with the life preservers, and the ballast that
was inclosed in the fish skin, she was constructed
so as to swim in the tank with her head and arms
and shoulders clear of the water, and with her back
hair, which was about 4 ft. long and genuine so far
as I know, floating out behind her.

"The agent filled up the tank with water, and the
Mermaid gave a performance, although she grumbled
a little at having to do it in cold water.   She would
swim around the tank singing to herself in some

sort of gibberish that the agent said was the Marquesas language. Then she would sit on an artificial rock in the middle of the tank and comb her hair, and cuss a little to herself, as I afterwards found out, because the hair, being wet, would get in

"THEN SHE WOULD SIT ON A ROCK AND COMB HER HAIR."

more or less of a tangle. Then she would keep on sitting on the rock while she would look at herself in a hand mirror, and sigh as if she thought she was beginning to grow grey and wrinkled, which she wasn't. Presently she would start as if she saw some particular young man in the audience, and with a wild shriek she would dive in the tank and swim around under water for about ten minutes as it seemed to me, though it was really only about four minutes. You see, she had begun her career as a Champion Woman Fish, and as such was accustomed to eat and smoke under the water. This Mermaid business was only an expansion, as you might say, of her original profession.

" ' What do you say to that ? ' asked the agent when the exhibition was over and the Mermaid had gone into my private office to get dry, and to put on her citizen's dress.

" Of course I told him that I didn't think much of it, but that I was willing to give the girl an engagement, provided she would take a nominal salary. From that we argued the thing for pretty near an hour, I being determined that such a first-class attraction shouldn't escape me, and he being bound to stick me for a salary that was about equal to that of an Eyetalian primer donner. We came to an agreement after a while, and all three went to dinner together. I will say that, for a professional, the Marquesas Mermaid was the most lady-like woman I have ever met, barring that she would drink more beer and whisky than, to my mind, a regular private lady would drink. But she said she had to do something to keep her blood circulating, and stave off the rheumatism, which was only reasonable, considering that she spent from three to four hours daily in her tank.

" Well! That Mermaid was the very biggest success I ever had, and I've had a good many since I first went into the business some thirty-seven years ago. About two-thirds of the people who came to see her believed in the Mermaid yarn, and the other third could not help admiring the splendid way in which she played her part, especially her performances under water. She was a remarkably well-behaved girl, too. She was always sober until after her day's work was done ; and if she did drink too much in her own bedroom, she never made a row and broke things, as a Fat Woman I once had who took to drink in consequence of a disappointment in love and broke seventy dollars worth of crockery, not to speak of tables and chairs, inside of three weeks.

" But there was one person who hated the Mermaid, and that was the Beautiful Circassian Girl. From the day the Mermaid came into the show the Circassian might as well have been out of it altogether, so far as attracting any attention went. Naturally she was jealous, as were all the other freaks, though

they did not show it so openly. The thing that
made the Circassian Girl the maddest was that the
Giant, who had been paying her attention 'for some
months, went clean over to the Mermaid, and hadn't
eyes in his head for any other girl.

"Now, the Circassian, who was a Spanish girl
from Cuba, and about as bad-tempered as they make

"THEY GOT UP A SCHEME."

'em, combined with the Dwarf, who was another
bad lot, and got up a scheme for getting square with
the Mermaid. They worked it in this way. The
girl was accustomed to stay in her tank for an hour
and a half at each performance, and of course we
had two performances a day. Naturally the water,

no matter how warm it might be at the start, would
grow cold in the course of an hour and a half, and
as it was late in the fall, and the weather was un-
seasonably cold, the Mermaid could not stand such
a change of temperature. So she had the tank
supplied with warm water that was heated in a
boiler in another room, and led into the tank by a
pipe. This kept the tank at an even temperature—
for the warm water was continually flowing into it,
while the overflow of cooler water ran off through
the escape pipe. She always saw for herself that the
water in the boiler was of the right temperature before her performance began, and took care that the
fire was brisk enough to keep the water properly
heated without overheating it.

"One afternoon the Dwarf pretended that he had
the rheumatism so bad that he couldn't show, and so
I gave him a day off. What does he do but hide himself in the room where the boiler was kept, and after the
Mermaid had seen that the fire was all right, and
had gone to her room to put on her Mermaid clothes,
he stirs up the fire, pours a lot of petroleum into the
coal-scuttle, and then fills up the furnace as full as
it would hold. After which he sneaked out, and
went to bed, pretending that he had been there all
day.

"The Mermaid went into her tank at 2·30 as usual, and as I was standing close to her at the time I noticed that she looked a little dissatisfied, the reason being, as I afterwards found out, that she thought the water was too hot to be quite comfort-

"HE STIRS UP THE FIRE."

able. She went through with the first part of her programme as usual: combing her hair, and singing in the Mermaid language, and swimming round the tank with her head and shoulders out of water, but all the time that look of dissatisfaction was

growing and spreading as you might say. Then
she came on to the second part of the programme,
in which she performed her submarine feats, and
no sooner had she sunk gracefully to the bottom of
the tank, than she came up to the surface again,
with the unhappiest expression I ever saw on a
woman's face. She supported herself by holding
on to the edge of the tank, and kept as much of herself out of the water as she could, and I could see
from the way that she looked at me that she was
dying to say something to me. It wouldn't do, however, for her to let the public suppose that she knew
how to speak any human language, so I just smiled
at her to encourage her, never thinking what the
real matter was.

" You see, the Dwarf had managed the fire so
that the water was by this time near up to the boiling point, and kept growing hotter every minute.
The girl stood it like a hero, and the perspiration
stood out all over her forehead. She kept moving herself around in the tank, trying to see if she
could strike a cooler section of the water, but it was
no use. The time came pretty soon when she had
to take her choice between being boiled and giving
herself away, and, naturally, she chose the latter.
At first she tried to get out of the tank without open-

ing her lips, but when she had swung herself up to
the rim of the tank, and was hanging over it, the
tank began to tip up, and presently the whole thing

"SHE SAID THAT SOME SCOUNDREL HAD TRIED TO BOIL HER."

went over with a crash and pretty near drowned the
people that were standing under it.

"The Mermaid, when she saw what was going
to happen, called out, 'Save me!' as loud as she
could, and when she was picked up, with her fish

skin extension burst open, and her feet showing through it, she knew the game was up, and she thought she might as well relieve her feelings with language. She stood up and made a speech to the public, saying that some scoundrel had tried to boil her, and threatening to kill him the first minute she could find him.

"I can overlook a good deal that people, and especially women, may say when they are excited, but the language the Mermaid used was really too much, and the public wouldn't stand it. As soon as they got over their first surprise they felt that they had been swindled, and they said so. It was a tough job for me to get the Mermaid away, and to get rid of the people. Of course, I had to give them their money back, but they said things about me that were very discouraging to a man whose living depends on the confidence that the public has in his honesty. That affair broke up my New York season, for I didn't dare to face the public again, and I just shut up shop and moved my company on to Philadelphia the next day.

"How did I find out that the Dwarf and the Circassian Girl had a hand in it? Why, because they naturally couldn't help bragging about it. However, I never said anything to them about it,

What was the use ? ' Let bad enough alone' is my motto. But I can tell you I kept a sharp eye on the Dwarf after that, and cured his rheumatism for him. The next time he came to me for a half holiday on account of rheumatism, I just said : ' You get into a tank of boiling water, and your rheumatism won't trouble you any more '. He knew what I was referring to, and he never said rheumatism to me again."

CHAPTER VIII.

THE BEAUTY SHOW.

" NEXT month," remarked the door-keeper, " I'm going to have a Beauty Show."

" Would you mind explaining," I asked, " why you should mix up beauties and freaks ? Do you mean to tell me that you consider a pretty woman a freak of Nature ? "

" It ain't a question of what you or I or anybody else considers," retorted the door-keeper. " A Beauty Show once in every three years is one of the traditions of the profession. It's more than three years since I had one, and I can't, in justice to myself, put it off any longer. I shall advertise for a dozen girls to-morrow, and next month or thereabouts I'll open my ' Grand Prize Contest of Beauty and Loveliness,' and I hope it will turn out better than my last one did."

" I don't want to be understood as reflecting on the beauty of Chicago women," said I ; " but I should think it would be difficult to find a dozen

beautiful women who would be willing to exhibit
themselves in that way."

"It ain't merely difficult; it's impossible," replied my friend. "But who wants a dozen beautiful women? If you understood the ins and outs of
the profession, you'd know that there is never but
one really handsome woman in a Beauty Show.
All the rest are fair to middling ugly, except one
who is as ugly as they make 'em. That's the
regular way of making up a Beauty Show, and it
wouldn't be the way unless it was sure to draw.

"You see," continued the door-keeper, "that the
public must be amused as well as instructed. You
go to work and give them a show consisting altogether of beautiful girls, and they'll, of course, be
instructed by it, but it won't amuse them a cent's
worth; whereas, if some of your girls are moder-
ately ugly, the public begins to smile at them for
imagining that they are handsome enough for a
Beauty Show; and when the public sees the girl
that is a holy terror of ugliness they laugh, and go
away and recommend all their friends to come and
see the show. You may say that it's a little rough
on the ugly girls to make a show of them; but so
long as they get their pay I don't see as they have
any cause to complain. Besides, they all believe

that they are handsome, and those who don't get the prizes think that they would have had a prize if the judges hadn't been fooled by that bold-faced, good-for-nothing girl who does get it. I've yet to see a woman in a Beauty Show who didn't consider herself a sort of Medecine Venus. Well, it's a blessed

"IT'S A LITTLE ROUGH ON THE UGLY GIRLS."

dispensation of Providence, for did you ever think how unhappy most women would be if they didn't have the consolation of thinking that they were beautiful ? "

" How do you manage about the prizes ? " I asked.

" Well, I appoint three disinterested judges, and tell them that the first prize must go to the handsome girl, and the second prize to the extra ugly girl ; and this arrangement always pleases the public. If the show draws well, I generally give a sort of consolation present to the rest of the girls— say a pocket-handkerchief apiece, or something of that sort, and, on the whole, they go away contented. I had one set of girls, though, and that was the last Beauty Show I had, who made things middling lively for me, and pretty well induced me to make up my mind that I'd never have another affair of the kind. But when you're once in the business you have to conform to the traditions of it, unless you're either a great genius or a blamed fool, and I try to be neither.

" Three years ago last January I opened a Beauty Show in this city. I wasn't at my present place at the time, for I was in a smaller hall down by the lake, and a mighty damp and unwholesome place it was. You couldn't keep a fat woman there without she'd lose flesh by the day ; and as for a giant, he'd be laid up with rheumatism more than half the time. However, the rent was low ; and I have to pay a rent where I am now that would break me if business should not be good.

" When I started to get up this Beauty Show that I'm telling you about, I advertised as usual, and was overrun with girls who wanted to be beauties at fifty cents a night. I selected my handsome girl without much difficulty ; for she was the only really good-looking girl out of the whole lot that applied. The only trouble was to select the one who was the ugliest. However, I got my dozen selected at last, and the show opened on a Monday, and promised to be a success. My handbills described the girls as ' Scions of the Most Aristocratic Families of the Great Metropolis of the West '. Of course, I knew that nobody would believe it, but the public expects to be lied to when a Beauty Show is in progress, and would be disappointed if you were to tell them the truth. A woman's looks is a subject that nobody is bound to tell the truth about. Suppose a married man were to try to tell the truth on such a subject! Where do you suppose his domestic happiness would go ?

" Theseyere girls were mostly working girls. They were all perfectly respectable or they couldn't have got into my show on any consideration ; but they were a little rough in their ways. I don't mind a little exchange of language, or a slap now and then ; but throwing lighted kerosene lamps is, in

9

my opinion, unladylike, and I won't allow it on my premises. It was the good looks of the girl that was meant to take the first prize that made all the others so raging against her that I had to have a man go with her and protect her every time she went from the museum to her own house. The other girls came to me the fourth day after we opened and said that I must discharge the good-looking girl—only they called her a very different name—or they would burst up my show. I said, ' Ladies ! One of the rules of this establishment is that I don't allow no cheek from nobody in my employ. You go back to your chairs and earn your wages, and take your chances of getting a prize. If you don't do this, you'll find yourselves in the street so sudden that you'll think there's been a dynamite explosion hereabouts, and you'll be asking the police to pick up your pieces.' You see, if you don't keep girls in their places they'll walk all over you. Perhaps you don't know this, not being, as you tell me, a married man, nor yet a man in any kind of show business. But what I'm telling you is the gospel truth, as you'll find out some day for yourself. Now these girls were in earnest, which is a very unusual thing for girls who talk about going on strike, or bursting up your business. They had made up their minds that the good-looking girl must go, and they weren't going to shrink from any means of carrying out this resolution. My lecturer—the chap who explains the tattooed girl, and such—came to me that afternoon, and told me that he was afraid that genuine mischief was brewing. So I told him I'd keep my weather eye lifting, and I didn't think any girls that could be got together in 'any hall in Chicago, no matter how big it might be, could get ahead of me. I just called an assistant and put him in charge of the door, and then went into the show to see what was going to happen.

"Nothing happened that afternoon, except that all the discontented girls took a great deal of pains to sit with their backs turned to the good-looking girl, and tittered whenever any one spoke to her. This didn't do any particular harm, and I made up my mind that there was nothing to be disturbed about. But that evening I had reason to change my mind.

"The Beauty Show lasted during the entire performance, and when the public were admitted they always found the beauties sitting in their chairs on the stage, pretending to read, or to be thinking of heaven with their eyes rolled up, looking at photographs of beloved objects, and fetching sighs every

now and then; in short, doing the regular things
that beauties in a Beauty Show are expected to do.
The evening I am speaking of, the public saw something that they had not expected to see.   The good-
looking girl was the same as usual, but all the other

"LYING BACK IN THEIR CHAIRS AS IF THEY WERE DEAD."

girls had painted their faces a dead white and their
lips sky blue, and were lying back in their chairs
as if they were dead.   They had calculated to scare
the public, and so burst my show up, but they got
badly left.   The public thought it was intended to
be comic, and they laughed and enjoyed themselves

to such an extent that I came in to see what was the matter, supposing, of course, that there was a free fight going on. After the performance was over, I told the girls that I was tremendously obliged to them for their addition to the performance, and that if they would do the same thing every night for a week, I would raise their salaries. Of course, they wouldn't do it, for they knew that they looked uglier than usual with their white faces and blue lips, and they saw that I was really pleased instead of being frightened. Finding that they could not induce me to discharge the good-looking girl by anything they could do, they called in the Dwarf, who had brains and malice enough to fit out half the women in Chicago, and told him they wanted him to invent some way of getting rid of the good-looking girl without actually killing her or disfiguring her for life.

" The Dwarf took to the notion at once, and pretty soon all sorts of things began to happen to that girl. One day, just as she was coming on to the stage, one of the other girls accidentally fell against her and put her hand against the good-looking girl's face, just to steady herself. Her hand was covered with soot ; and when the public came in, they found the good-looking girl sitting and smiling at them with the dirtiest face a man ever saw on a woman outside of a coal mine. Another day she found a mouse tied to the leg of her chair with a horse-hair; and as she couldn't see the horse-hair, she naturally thought that her last day had come, and fainted away then and there. Another day the Dwarf stole the bottle that she always kept in the dressing-room, and that held something that she used to put on her hair, to give it a good shine; and he filled the bottle up with some chemical that I don't pretend to know the name of, but that he got from a friend of his who was in the chemical line. The good-looking girl put it on her hair, and in about twenty minutes her hair had turned a deep blue. That amused the public and disgusted the girl; and if she hadn't taken my advice to dye her hair yellow, which really improved her appearance, she would probably have given up and withdrawn to private life.

"I say the Dwarf was at the bottom of all these little games, though it never could be proved against him. That was his way. He could do more different kinds of devilment, and let all the world know he did it, while all the time he would manage to make it impossible for anybody to prove anything against him legally. He had all the advantages of a big reputation for wickedness, without any of the disadvantages; and if he had been a full-sized man, decent folks like you and I, would have had no kind of chance compared with him among the women. The cashier of one of our leading banks said to me one day, ' That Dwarf of yours is a wonderful fellow. If he was a cashier he'd manage to carry off every cent of the money, without having to go to Canada like the rest of us. He'd just stay right here and spend the money, and nobody could prove the first thing against him.' I mention this to show the sort of estimation that our leading men had of him —and he deserved it.

" The good-looking girl stood the persecution. of the others until the show had only about two more weeks to run, and then she gave it up, and for a pretty good reason. The chairs on which the beauties sat were screwed down to the floor, so as to keep the girls from hitching up close to one another, and gossiping and neglecting their duty. They were plain wooden chairs, for I'm not one of those who believe that the public can be attracted by up-holstery instead of genuine merit. I leave that sort of thing to theatrical managers. They can bring out Shakespeare with real velvet furniture, and third-rate actors, if they want to, but I prefer to spend my

money in first-class talent, and let the talent sit in
plain and inexpensive chairs.

"One Sunday afternoon I was passing through
the auditorium, and I noticed a slight smell of varnish. Of course I asked what it meant, and the
Dwarf told me that the Giant had been varnishing
his helmet. So I thought no' more about it, supposing that the Dwarf had told the truth, which he
had been known to do, or at any rate suspected of
doing, several times during the nine years that he
had been with me. But the Dwarf was lying about
the Giant, who had never touched the varnish. It
was the Dwarf himself, who had laid in a pot of
varnish so thick that it would take a week to dry,
and so sticky that you could have almost mended a
broken leg with it. He had laid this varnish on to
the seat and back of the good-looking girl's chair,
and as it was perfectly transparent he knew the girl
wouldn't see it. As for smelling it, she had a cold
in the head, and couldn't have smelt a New York
street if you had set her down in the middle of it on
an August day.

"All the other girls were in their places before
the good-looking girl came on the stage that afternoon, and when she did come not one of them looked
at her. She sat down and smiled as usual at the

public; but by-and-by they began to notice that she didn't seem quite easy. She seemed to want to move round in her chair without being entirely able to do it. Things went along until about the middle of the performance, when all the girls had to stand up in a row and sing a song about Heaven being their home, and that sort of thing, which always takes better with the general public than the best comic song. The rest of the girls accordingly stood up, but the good-looking girl didn't move, and people thought that she was some sort of infidel, and openly said that she ought to be ashamed of herself. Well, the girls got through with their singing and sat down again, and presently in comes the Dwarf, and goes round and whispers to one after another of the girls. He afterwards told me that he had smelt smoke, and thinking that the place might be on fire, he had warned the girls to get out of it quietly, so as not to make a panic. Each girl as he whispered to her put on a look of horror, and slid out of the door at the back of the stage, until it came to the good-looking girl, who was the last one to be told of the pretended fire. The poor thing was frightened half out of her mind. She tried her best to wrench herself out of her chair, and her clothes tore here and there, but they held her all the same. She

saw that she could never pull herself loose without
leaving the bulk of her clothes behind her, and being a respectable girl, she couldn't bring her mind
to do this. Just then she saw me in the crowd, and

"THE POOR THING WAS FRIGHTENED HALF OUT OF HER MIND."

beckoned to me. Of course, I saw that something
serious was the matter, and when I went up to her
and she begged me to drop the curtain if I didn't
want her to die of fright and be burned to death as
well, I did what she wanted. Then, when I found

out how things stood, I sent for the Strong Woman to pull the girl loose, and I lent her my ulster. She went home in a cab and sent in her resignation that very evening.

"I wound that Beauty Show up the next day, and arranged with the judges that the good-looking girl should take both the first and second prizes. The other girls I paid off, giving them just their wages and no more, and as for the Dwarf, I told him that he needed a larger sphere for his talents, and recommended him to go into politics, seeing as he had just the elements for making a successful statesman. So you see my last Beauty Show wasn't altogether satisfactory to me. But what is satisfactory here below? You probably envy me because I have the most prosperous Dime Museum in the country; but I can tell you there are times when I'd be glad to change places with a country Methodist preacher, with a big family, and a salary not a quarter the size of my average weekly receipts."

CHAPTER IX.

THE BABY SHOW.

"Speaking of Beauty Shows," said I to my friend the door-keeper, as we were having our usual night-cap together, after we had finished with the business of the day; "did you ever have a Baby Show?"

"Did I ever understand my profession?" returned the door-keeper disdainfully. "Why, man, a Baby Show is what the public expect at least once in every six years; and if you are going to disappoint the public, you'd better go out of the Dime Museum business, and become a professional reformer at once. Yes, sir; I've had Baby Shows, and I'll have to have more of them if I live. But I am free to say to you, it being between old friends—for, some-how, I've got to look on you as an old friend, and have given you all the ins and outs of my profession. You might be intending to go into the profession yourself, and you might have been pumping me all this time just with the intention of using my infor-mation in a way to help yourself, at my expense.

(130)

But I'm a pretty good judge of men, and I don't believe you're that sort of a man."

He paused, forgetful of the fact that his original sentence had run off the track, so to speak, and had arrived nowhere. "You were saying that you felt free to say something about Baby Shows, but you forgot to tell me what it was," I remarked.

" That's a fact," replied the door-keeper. " What I was going to say was this—that a Baby Show is, in my opinion, the very meanest and most unsatisfactory thing a manager can possibly tackle. Why, I had rather have four rival Circassian Beauties in my show at one time, than have a Baby Show. And if you had ever seen four rival Circassian Beauties together—threatening to pull out one another's hair, and aching to destroy one another's complexions— you'd understand what I mean.

"I once had a nephew with me who wanted to learn the business, and thought he knew it all before he had been with me two weeks. Perhaps I've mentioned it before. I don't talk much about my family, as a rule, and I despise a man who is always bragging of his relations ; but I will say that this nephew of mine was the biggest idiot, considered as a business man, you understand, that I ever heard of in the whole course of my professional career.

I've known some pretty substantial fools in my time, especially in the days when I ran a Spiritual Medium business; but, for sudden bursts of genius in the line of idiocy, thishyer nephew of mine laid over any regular idiot I ever struck.

"One day he came to me and said, ' Uncle ! You say you are going to have a Baby Show. I want you to give the management of it over to me, just so as you can see how well I understand the business.' I didn't know at that time to what lengths of foolishness he could go, and just by way of experiment, for I always had a scientific turn, I thought I would let him try what he could do. So I told him to go ahead, and exhibit himself with the babies, if he wanted to do it. I knew the babies wouldn't feel hurt; they didn't have sense enough to understand what being put on a level with my nephew meant.

"Well, Jerry—that was my nephew's name— went ahead, and engaged a dozen babies in the course of the next few days. It's an easy job to collect your babies when you have a Baby Show. You go into the poorest tenement houses in the city, and you can hire a thousand babies at fifty cents a week without the least trouble. Of course, among the thousand there would be, say eight hundred, that would be too thin and sickly to be fit for exhibition ; but their mothers would be all the more glad to put them where they would get good food for a week, and not be eating their heads off at the same time.

" Most managers when they get up a Baby Show engage the mothers to appear on the stage and take care of their kids. Now, when you remember the class of people who put their babies into Baby Shows, you can see that the babies' mothers are not likely to be an attraction in the eyes of the public. This is one of the drawbacks of the show ; and as three or four of the mothers are generally middling full of gin, they are sure to give the manager a lot of trouble. The truth is, the whole system of Baby Shows is nothing but trouble and vexation ; but it goes to prove what is one of the great fundamental principles of the show business, and that is that the public will look at anything, provided they have to pay to do it.

" There isn't a pleasant day in the whole year when there isn't at least a hundred more or less babies in the Park, where anybody can see them for nothing. Did you ever hear of a man who cared to stop and look at free babies in the Park ? Of course you never did. But you just take and put a dozen

commonplace babies in a Dime Museum, and charge
ten cents admission, and the public will crowd to
see them.   It's my belief that if you were to charge
an admission fee to every church service, the very
men who never think of hearing a sermon now-a-
days, would rush to pay their money and listen to a
sermon two hours long.   I recommended this plan
to a friend of mine, who is the pastor of the Twenty-
fifth Eighth Day Baptist Church in Cincinnati, and
he said he believed I had hit on the true way of fill-
ing up the waste places of Zion.

   " What was I saying about thishyer Baby Show ?
Something about the mothers ?   Yes ; I remember,
now.   Well, seeing what a nuisance the mothers
generally are, Jerry decided he wouldn't have any of
them in the show.   So he hired six young girls to
act as nurses ; and, as they were pretty girls to start
with, and were dressed in a nice uniform, they
promised to form an independent attraction, of which
Jerry was particularly proud.

   " The mothers were to bring their babies to the
show and have them regularly entered, and then
they were to have no more to do with them until
the show was over.   This suited them very well ;
though they said it was awfully cruel, and stood
out for ten cents a day additional pay on the ground

that their maternal instincts were outraged—and got it, too. The nurses were real, genuine nurse-girls, who understood how to take care of babies. That I saw to myself; for I wasn't going to have half a

"THEY WERE PRETTY GIRLS."

dozen babies die on my hands, and have to pay damages for them.

" The morning the show was to begin the mothers brought their kids, and Jerry received them. He numbered every baby, and entered it in a book. For

10

instance, baby No. 1 was entered as belonging to Mrs. Smith, and baby No. 2 to its proper mother, and so on. Then Jerry marked the number of each baby on the small of its back, with a paint brush and some black varnish that would dry inside of five minutes; and when the figures were dry, he turned the babies over to the nurses, and told them to wash them and dress them in pretty little white dresses that he had provided at my expense.

"The Baby Show opened at two o'clock that afternoon, and the women said it was a holy and beautiful sight. Each baby had a small cradle to itself, and sat up with its bottle on its lap, and its little stomach comfortably full for the first time probably in its miserable little life. I will say that they were a remarkably well-behaved set of babies. Whether it was that they were healthier than the general run of exhibition babies, or whether the nurses knew how to manage them better than the average mother does, or whether the particular food for infants that we gave them met their views better than ordinary milk, I can't say. All I know is that they very seldom howled, or complained of pins or anything of that sort, and accordingly the nurses had time to get in a good deal of work for them-

selves. Three of the lot were engaged to be married
before the show was over, and the rest of them had
an average of five admirers each hanging round
them all the time. Each nurse had two babies to
take care of, and this was a useful experience for
her, in case she should ever be visited by twins, and
we never know in this world what may happen to
us.

" The babies were only exhibited from two to five
o'clock each day, and were then put to sleep for the
rest of the night. Every morning the nurses washed
them ; and, judging from the sounds that used to
come out of the nursery while this was going on, the
girls regarded it as the best sort of fun. The show
drew well, and I couldn't see as my nephew had
made any mistake in the matter. I really began to
hope that he might develop some sort of an intellect if he stayed with me long enough; and
when he used to come to me in the evening after
we had closed our doors, and would say, ' Well,
uncle, do I understand how to run a Baby Show,
or don't I ? ' I couldn't see my way to answering
him except by admitting that the show was doing
remarkably well. He grew more and more con-
ceited every day, and used to spend his leisure time
telling the Giant, who was a weak-minded sort of

chap, what tremendous improvements a man of real genius could make in the Dime Museum business, and how he was the identical man who was going to make them.   He didn't talk that way quite so much after the Baby Show was over.

"We took in, that week, three hundred and seventeen dollars and twenty cents more than our average receipts, and there is no danger that I will ever forget it, for my nephew, after we had quarrelled, and he had left me—going out of the back window neck and crop—for, when it comes to chucking a man out, I'm there all the time, and don't you forget it!—he sent me a summons for three hundred and seventeen dollars and twenty cents, with interest thereon from the eleventh day of June, 1879, together with the costs of this action.   Of course, I didn't pay it, but I had to go to court and waste time and money, besides employing a lawyer.   It was like his cheek, to claim that the receipts of the Baby Show belonged to him, considering what he made me pay the mothers for damages, all through his mismanagement.

"I said that the particular kind of infants' food that the babies took seemed to agree with them. It was furnished gratis as an advertisement by the company that sold it, and every baby had a placard

fastened to its cradle, which said, ' This infant is
fed exclusively on Jones' Food for Infants '. What
with having nourishing food, and plenty of it, and
nothing to harass their minds, the babies grew fat by
the day, and the nurses used to say that they didn't
believe their mothers would know them when the
time to return them should come round.

" I told you of Jerry's bright idea of putting the
number of each infant on its back with black varnish.
This was the means by which he expected to identify
them when the time came to close the show ; but,
if he had known more about babies, he would have
remembered that they are washed every morning,
and that black varnish is no better than the indelible
ink that folk use to mark their linen, and that it is
bound to come off in the wash. What with the
nurses being very faithful in the matter of washing,
which, of course, resulted in the black marks being
carefully washed away, and what with their habit
of changing babies every day or two, just to put a
little variety into their occupation, it came to pass
that when the show closed, and Jerry told the nurses
that the mothers would come to take their babies
back at six o'clock sharp, there wasn't a blessed
nurse who had the least idea which baby was which.

" When one of the nurses asked Jerry how the

babies were to be identified, and it came out in the course of the conversation that followed that the marks had been washed off the babies, and that nobody could possibly tell who the different babies belonged to, Jerry began to doubt whether he was such a tremendous able manager after all. I happened to be on hand at the time and heard all about it, but I didn't undertake to advise my nephew. It was his funeral, and I didn't want to interfere with the corpse. I could see that he was a good deal troubled, and that the nurses—who didn't like him very well—were a good deal amused at his predicament. They knew what tenement-house mothers are, as a general thing, and they knew there would be a pretty lively sort of circus when the mothers come to claim their infants.

"Jerry, however, put a bold face on it, and got rid of the nurses before the mothers arrived. When the mothers were all present—except two, who had been locked up during the week, and had sent their husbands in their places, Jerry brought out the babies one by one; and, after making a great show of looking in his ledger, so as to make no mistake about identifying them, he gave each woman a baby, together with fifty cents more pay than he had promised her—he hoping, in this way, that she would

"THE WOMEN DIDN'T SEEM TO HAVE THE FIRST BIT OF MATERNAL INSTINCT."

be too much pleased with the money to take particular notice of her kid. But the scheme failed.
There wasn't a mother who didn't swear that she
had the wrong baby, and at one time it looked to me
—who was acting as a disinterested spectator—that
Jerry was going to come out of the affair with less
hair on his head than a young man of his age would
like to have. However, he finally proposed that
the women should select their own babies, which
was accordingly agreed to. This led to their
quarrelling among themselves instead of quarrelling
with him, but it didn't bring the matter to any sort
of settlement. The women didn't seem to have the
first bit of maternal instinct, so far as knowing their
own infants was concerned. It may be a wise child
that knows its own father, but it would be a great
sight wiser mother who could pick out her own baby
from among a dozen babies of the same age, and
dressed just alike. There wasn't a single woman
who was allowed to select a baby without some
other woman putting in a claim for it, and there
were three babies that were so popular that there
were six or seven claimants for each of them.

" There didn't seem to be any way of satisfying
the women, and Jerry just sat in a helpless sort of
way, waiting for the trouble to blow over, which it

declined to do. Two of the women chose what they considered to be the best babies, and made off with them ; and when they were fairly gone, the very women who had laid claim to those identical babies, said they had been mistaken, and swore that two of the next best quality of babies were the ones that belonged to them. It was just for all the world like choosing umbrellas at a swell party. The idea was to get the best baby, if you could ; and if not, to get the next best.

"I told you there were two men who came for babies, their wives being at the time unavoidably detained in the county gaol. They took no part in the disturbance. Now and then they would remark, 'Ladies! please remember that we've got a claim on two of them there kids, and after you've satisfied yourselves we'd like to take a hand in the proceedings ourselves,' but nobody paid any attention to them. After a while, however, one of the men says, 'That there black-eyed baby is mine, if I ain't mistaken. Anyhow, I'm going to take it,' and with that he picks up a middling valuable infant, and was just going to leave, when a woman throws herself screaming on him, and begins to tear his eyes out, on the ground that he was kidnapping her child. So I stepped out and asked the policeman on our beat to come in and straighten things out. He didn't like the job very much, but he was a mighty intelligent man, and when he saw how things were going he proposed a compromise, which was, in his opinion, the only way to settle the matter. He advised the women to put each baby up to be voted for, and that the question of its ownership should be settled by a majority vote. The women agreed, but when seven women voted that the baby claimed by Mrs. O'Flaherty did not belong to her, and only Mrs. O'Flaherty voted that it did—the two men not being asked to take part in the proceedings—it was clear that the policeman's plan was going to be a failure. Then he proposed, being a popular man with the ladies, and being well known to the two men, through having often showed them the way to the station-house, that he himself should act as umpire, and decide how the babies were to be divided. The policeman added that he knew the liberal character of the Colonel—meaning me, of course—and that he was sure that I was ready to stand beer for all the mothers who might feel themselves disappointed. The women, seeing as they could not think of any other way of settling the difficulty, agreed to his proposal, and the policeman began his task.

" First, he called up Mrs. O'Flaherty, and asked

her what colour her baby's eyes and hair were, and
then he selected a baby of that general description
and handed it over to her.   There was some little
grumbling from the women, but not much, for most
of them had their minds fixed on the beer that was
to console them, and they thought their best plan
was to put on an air of heart-broken sadness, and to
keep quiet.   The two men were served with babies
last of all, as was to be expected in a country where
everybody is polite to the ladies.   They naturally
were put off with the most undesirable infants, but
only one of them objected.   He said to the policeman, ' Sor ! when me child was sent here he was a
fine boy av the name of Pathrick.   Sor ! I do not go
for to find fault with your decision, but if what this
good lady on me right says is the truth there has
been foul play somewheres, for this child, which you
say is me boy Pathrick, is nothing more nor less
than a girl, and it's meself that'll have throuble explaining of the change to me wife when her time is
up.'   But the policeman told him he couldn't interfere in anybody's domestic affairs, and that, having
once made his decision concerning the ownership of
the babies, he couldn't change it to accommodate
any man's prejudices.   The upshot was that after
I had ordered in a quart of beer for every woman

and man of them, the whole gang went away, still arguing a little with one another about their babies, but, on the whole, pretty well satisfied.

"That wasn't the last of it, however. The next day, not a mother of them all was contented. They kept coming to me and demanding money for having lost their babies, and as I knew the thing would get into the papers if I didn't stop their mouths, and would do me a lot of injury, I paid them in the end pretty near as much as the whole Baby Show had brought in. As for my nephew, I dismissed him the day after the show, and it was his fault that he didn't take his dismission quietly, and save me from having to chuck him out. No, sir ! I don't like Baby Shows, and I am living in hopes that some of these philanthropic societies, that won't allow a child to earn an honest living on the stage, will manage to get a bill through the legislature prohibiting Baby Shows. Such a bill would make the profession a great deal pleasanter, to a man who loves quiet, than it is now."

CHAPTER X.

THE LIGHTNING CALCULATOR.

" I SEE by your advertisement," I said to the door-keeper, "that you have a Lightning Calculator. Do you class Lightning Calculators as freaks?"

" Some of them ought to be classed as frauds," replied my friend, " but professionally they belong 'Among the Freaks'."

" Tell me," I continued, "how does a man become a Lightning Calculator?   Is he born such, or does he achieve lightning calculation?"

" Well! some of them are men that are born chock-full of figures. This sort are mostly Scotchmen, and they naturally learn the business easy. But most of the Lightning Calculators that I have known have been men with good memories, considerable brains, and a lot of cheek.   Now, you could make a good Lightning Calculator with about six months' study. It's by no means a difficult line. You begin by learning to add up columns of figures two and three at a time, and in a little while you

can add a column of thousands in less time than
another man could add a column of tens. Then, for
the square root racket, you just commit to memory
all the square roots of everything up to a hundred,
and you can do the same with cube roots. Then
when a man asks you the square root of say 9867,
you just give him the square root of ninety-eight,
with a thundering lot of decimals, and it makes no
sort of difference if the decimals are right or wrong.
Any man with a little memory, and a good deal of
cheek, can do the root business in a way that will
fill the public with admiration. You see it isn't
allowed to ask the Lightning Calculator any questions that are in any of the arithmetics, because, as
you explain, he might have committed the answers
to memory ; but the questions must be made up on
the spot. Nobody can find out while the show is
going on whether the Lightning Calculator's answers
are right or wrong, so he has only to keep cool, and
his chance of being caught out is pretty small.
Mind, I don't positively say this is the way all
Lightning Calculators work their game, for I never
asked one of them anything about his professional
secrets, but it's the way, I imagine, that most of
them practise.

"You may go to every Dime Museum in the

country and you'll never see a Female Calculator.
This always used to strike me as rather queer, until
I tried to bring out a Female Lightning Calculator,
and then I learned why no woman has ever succeeded at the business.

" The way it happened was like this : I had a
Lightning Calculator—Jim Slazey was his name—
who was about as smart as they make 'em ; much
too smart, in fact, for his own good. He was popular among the rest of my company, for he had considerable money, and was always standing beer, and
sympathising with what he called the wrongs of the
employed. One day the Dwarf came to me and
said, ' Colonel, I am delegated to give you notice
that on Monday next we are all going to leave you '.

" ' What's up ? ' said I. ' Don't I treat you well
enough, or are you thinking of setting up in private
life as millionaires ? '

" ' We've no fault to find with our treatment, as
far as that goes,' said the Dwarf, ' but we think that
there ain't no reason why you should make so much
money and we should make so little. We're going
to run this show on the co-operative principle, and
we shall offer you the place of treasurer and door-
keeper, for we want a square man for that position,
and we know you are honest, whatever else you

may be. We are prepared to give you fifty dollars a week, and I think that is a pretty handsome offer.'

" ' So do I,' I answered. ' I'll take the place and try to earn your approval. But, in the meantime, would you mind telling me how you came to find out how much money I am making ? '

" ' It was the Lightning Calculator that showed us how things are,' said the Dwarf. ' When he goes in for figures there is no mistake about him. He gets there every time. Now last night you had a good average house, and the Calculator says that there were four hundred people here in the afternoon, and five hundred and eighty-two in the evening. At ten cents each that makes over ninety-two dollars. I've got it all written down on this paper, so there can't be any mistake about it. Now, ninety-two dollars a day, is five hundred and fifty-two dollars a week, without counting the extra large houses that you generally have on Saturdays. Say your rent is twenty dollars a week, and your lights and fires are twenty more. Then add to this your salary list, which is exactly three hundred and ten dollars. This leaves you a weekly profit of about two hundred dollars a week, and we think that might just as well be divided among us, who bring in the money.'

" 'All right,' says I.   'Next Monday we'll begin
the co-operative plan, and Saturday night you can
see how you like it.'

" Next Monday the freaks undertook to manage
things. They did a good deal of quarrelling over
the programme, for everybody wanted to about
double the length of his or her act, and the first programme they drew up would have occupied about
thirty-six hours. The Fat Woman wanted to do a
song and dance act, and cried when they wouldn't
let her do it on the ground that the stage wasn't
strong enough; and the Wild Man of Borneo wanted
to end his performance by reading an original poem,
though, as a rule, I am told that wild men in Borneo
don't write poems in the English language, whatever wild men in England or America may do.
But after a while they came to some sort of agreement, and the programme remained pretty much as
I had made it.

" Saturday night the Dwarf came to the ticket
office, after the show was over, to count the house,
and when he found that there were only three
hundred and twelve tickets, he said there was something wrong, for the Lightning Calculator had
counted four hundred and seven people in the house.

" 'I don't deny that,' said I.   'But he forgot all

about the free list. We've got a thundering big free list that averages about one-fourth of the entire attendance. You can't run this sort of show without it; unless you want to be denounced in all the papers as demoralising the young and corrupting the old.'

" The Dwarf admitted that I was right about the free list ; and then he wanted to know just how much money would be coming to the Co-operated Freaks.

" ' After deducting my fifty dollars,' said I, 'and deducting the running expenses, there will be about seventeen dollars deficit, which you will, of course, make up to me. You forgot another little item. I give you all your board and lodging, which you couldn't possibly get anywhere else for ten dollars a week apiece. This has got to be added to your expenses, unless, of course, you all mean to show yourselves as Fasting Men and Fasting Women. You can't expect your door-keeper to feed and lodge you for nothing.'

" The Dwarf studied over the thing a while, and then he went and consulted his companions. The result was that he came back and said that they had had enough of co-operation, and would go back to their original system of drawing salaries. I agreed

to this, though, as a matter of fact, I should have
made more money on a salary of fifty dollars a week,
which was more than my average profits.   The
Lightning Calculator I discharged the next day, telling him that he calculated more freely than I cared
to have any one do who was in my employ.   And
then I set out to find another Calculator to take his
place.

"There was living in Chicago at the time, a girl
who had been with me some years before as a Circassian Beauty.   She had left the business because
it didn't give room for her intellect, which was the
biggest intellect I ever knew any girl to have.   The
fact was she was over-engined, and that made her a
little cranky at times.   She had some money of her
own, and she had only gone on the stage as a Circassian Beauty through love of the profession.   It
occurred to me that she was just the sort of woman
who could succeed as a Lightning Calculator, and
that a Female Lightning Calculator would be a sure
draw.   So I went to see her and we fixed the thing
up in no time.

"She thought at first that she couldn't learn the
racket, but when I explained to her how simple it
was, and that the chief thing needed was cheek, she
said she could do it.   I gave her the general outlines

of the thing, and told her to take plenty of time and
study it up till she could be sure not to make a
failure on the stage, and then I went back to my
place feeling pretty sure that I had struck a good
thing.

"That girl worked day and night, for at the beginning she didn't know any more about figures
than an ordinary woman, and that is precious little,
as you probably know yourself, if you are a married
man. It's a mighty curious thing how figures
always throw a woman. They can learn to add up
a column as quick, and almost as straight as a man,
but the trouble is that they can never learn to keep
things separate, and are always adding together
things that don't belong together. But women are
curious in a great many respects, and the man who
has spent forty years in a Dime Museum and still
can't feel that he knows all about them, is a living
proof that a woman is, as King Solomon says, something that no fellow can find out.

"In about a month the girl came to me and said
she was letter perfect, and could calculate any Male
Lightning Calculator clean out of sight. I tried her
with a few simple things, and found that she could
do them like a flash. I tried simple things, you
understand, because they have to be done right,

whereas the square roots and such are mostly guess-work, and any one can do them.

"When the time came for her first appearance in public, I gave her a first-class advertisement, and the posters, which showed her in red and yellow

"I GAVE HER A FIRST-CLASS ADVERTISEMENT."

tights, calculating with her back-hair down, were alone worth the price of admission. Of course, she didn't calculate in tights, but you've got to allow a little artistic licence in your posters, for you can't tie an artist—one of those that makes pictures, you understand—down to bare facts. The novelty of a Female Lightning Calculator took with the public, as I expected it would, and when she made her deebutt there was no sort of standing room left in the house.

"My former Lightning Calculator—Jim Slazey —the one who was discharged for calculating with too free a hand, was still hanging around the town waiting for an engagement, and, not finding it, he naturally came to see my Female Calculator. She began well, and added up and subtracted rows of figures at a rate that beat the best time of any previous Calculator. After a little she came to the place in the programme where the audience was asked to set sums for her to add up, and there's where my former Calculator got in his nefarious work.

"'If you please, ma'am,' said he, 'I'd like to have you do this sum. Add three thousand, nine hundred and seventy-eight dogs to five thousand, eight hundred and fifty-six cats, and tell me what the answer will be.'

"Quick as lightning, the Female Calculator answered, 'Nine thousand, eight hundred and thirty-four'.

"'Right,' says Jim, 'but nine thousand, eight hundred and thirty-four what?'

" ' Why cats, I suppose,' said the girl.

" ' So you mean to say that you can convert dogs into cats by adding them together, do you ? ' asked the chap, in a sneering voice.

" ' Well, then there are nine thousand and odd dogs,' said the Female Calculator.

" ' No, there ain't neither,' said the man, who I could now see was intending to put the girl in a hole. ' You're a long way off, ma'am. Adding cats and dogs together don't make either cats or dogs.'

" ' Then what does it make ? ' asked the girl.

" ' It just makes the liveliest sort of row, as you'll find if ever you try it,' said Jim.

" At this the people began to laugh, and the villain was encouraged to go on with his cussedness.

" ' I will now ask you,' said he, ' another simple question. Add five thousand, six hundred and seventeen pounds of flour to thirty gallons of water, one pound of salt, and ninety-nine eggs, and tell me the result.'

" The girl hesitated a minute, and then she said, ' Five thousand, seven hundred and forty-seven '.

" ' That's right enough, so far as figures go,' said the villain, ' but what do you call the result ? Just give it a name, will you ? '

" The girl did not know what to say. She rather thought the result was flour, but she wasn't sure about it. So she thought she would risk it, and said it was ' Five thousand, seven hundred and forty-seven eggs '.

" This time the people didn't wait for any further explanation, but laughed till the poor girl turned pale, and began to lose her nerve.

" ' I see,' said my old Calculator, as cool and cruel as an inspector of a gas-meter; ' you're not quite the sort of Lightning Calculator that the public requires. No, ma'am! that there simple sum when added up don't make eggs. It makes the pizonest kind of cake, as you'll find if ever anybody risks - housekeeping with you, and you try to make cake for him.

" ' We will now proceed,' said the wretch, ' to do a few small sums in simple subtraction. To begin, I will ask you to tell me what is left when you take twenty-seven thousand, three hundred and eighty-one pair of trousers, from twenty-eight hundred thousand, seven hundred and thirty-eight men ? '

" ' Thirteen hundred and fifty-seven,' said the girl.

" ' Please tell us what thishyer thirteen hundred and odd would be,' continued her tormentor.

" ' Why, they'd be men, of course,' said the girl, feeling sure she was right.

" ' But there were twenty-eight hundred thousand, seven hundred and thirty-eight men to begin with. What's become of all the missing ones ? '

" The girl reflected a bit, and then, half crying, said that she couldn't exactly say.

" ' Folks that set up to be Lightning Calculators ought to be able to answer the simplest kind of questions in subtraction,' said Jim. ' I'll tell you what has become of them. They have all gone into the house to put on other trousers.   See ? '

" The girl said that she hadn't come there to be insulted, and that if anybody was going to ask her any more questions, they must be decent ones.

" ' All right,' said the fellow, who was in the best of spirits, seeing as how the girl was losing her head, ' we'll bar trousers, if you consider them improper.   Now tell me, if you can, what is left when you take three hundred and six young men away from seven hundred and four girls. You see I have given you only a three-column sum, since you don't seem to be quite up to four-column sums.'

" ' There would be three hundred and ninety-eight girls left,' was the answer.

" ' You're quite sure about that, are you ? Very well. Perhaps you'll kindly tell us where the other three hundred and six girls have gone ? '

" ' They haven't gone anywhere,' said the girl.

" ' But there were seven hundred and four of them before they lost their young men,' persisted Jim. ' Do you mean to tell me that more than half of them have been just wiped out ? '

" The girl didn't say anything, but stood and glared at Jim.

" ' Well,' said he, ' I see that subtraction is too much for you. I'll try you with a little multiplication. If you multiply seven million, nine hundred and twelve boys by three hundred thousand mince pies, what do you get ? '

" ' If you're going to ask me any more questions just you step up here on the stage, and write 'em down on the blackboard,' said the girl.

" ' Just as you please,' said Jim ; and with that he steps up on the stage and begins to write down his figures, turning, of course, his back to the girl while he was doing it. Before he had got fairly started, she had him by the hair with one hand, and was cuffing his ears with the other.

" ' I can't add nothing, can't I ? ' she yelled at him. ' You add all them cuffs together, and see how much they make. I can't do no substraction neither, can't I? How much hair will you have left after I get through substracting it?' and with

"I CAN'T ADD NOTHING, CAN'T I?"

that she rakes out a handful of hair, and gets a fresh hold of his whiskers. 'You'll come here with your fool questions, will you?' she continued; 'I'll learn you how to do Lightning Calculating!' and she fetches him one on the nose that started the claret very lively.

" I judged it was about time for me to interfere, so I just took Jim by the scruff of the neck, and ran him out of the show, while the people gave three cheers for the girl, and three more for me. But it was too late. As a Lightning Calculator she was ruined. She offered to extract square roots, and all that, but nobody cared to listen to her, and she went home weeping. The next day she threw up her engagement, which saved me the trouble of breaking it, for she was a dead failure, and I couldn't possibly have kept her on.

" Now you can see why a woman can never succeed as a Lightning Calculator. They can never learn that you mustn't add different kinds of things together. It's what the scientific chaps call an idiotsyncracy, and you can't get it out of a woman, no matter how much pains you may take with her."

CHAPTER XI.

AN AMATEUR JUGGLER.

ONE evening I asked the door-keeper whether juggling was as popular an attraction as it formerly was, for I remembered how, in my boyish days, a juggler was even more wildly fascinating than a pantomime.

"I can't tell you much about Jugglers," he replied; "they are not in my line. You'll very seldom see a Juggler in a Dime Museum, and when you do see him, he is not a legitimate attraction. In order to be a Juggler, a man has got to have intellects into him; whereas, the less intellects a freak has, the better for him and his manager. You can see for yourself that it don't require any intellect to be a Fat Woman, or a Giant, but, in my opinion, it's a higher branch of the theatrical profession. Any ordinary man can learn to play Shakespeare, or to do tricks with cards, but it's one man in a hundred thousand that can stand six feet six in his stockings. It's the same way with women. Any ordinary woman who has a rich husband can go on the stage and play Juliet, and Lady Macbeth, and such, but ask her to bring her weight up to four hundred pounds, and you'll find she can't do it. I tell you, it's a mistake for any one to look down on the Dime Museum business, and class it, as everybody does, below the legitimate drama. On the contrary, I consider it a high-class entertainment, and I've been in the business long enough to be a judge. When it comes to understanding the Dime Museum business from top to bottom, there ain't no flies on me, and don't you forget it."

The door-keeper was silent for a few minutes after this burst of eulogy of his profession, and then he added : —

"I did once or twice have a Juggler in my show, when things were rather slack, and I wanted something to stir the public up, but I couldn't see as much ever came of it. There was an amachure, though, who once paid me twenty-five dollars to take the regular Juggler's place for one night only, and he made things particularly lively.

"The regular Juggler was old Yung Ling, the celebrated Chinese Prestidigitator, and, of course, you've heard of him. No? Well, you surprise me, especially seeing as you are an Englishman. Yung

Ling was an Englishman, too—one of those chaps
that keeps heaving his aitches into his conversation
without caring a rap what they may fasten to. He
used to have a way of painting his eyes so as to
give them a slope, that made him the picture of a
Chinaman ; and unless you saw him after business
hours, with his face washed and a briarwood
pipe in his mouth, and he arguing in favour of giving
up Trafalgar Square to cheap shows on Sunday afternoons, you would never dream that he was anything
else but a genuine Chinaman. He was a good
Juggler, too, one of the very best in the profession—
that is in the days before Maskelyne & Cooke
took to mixing juggling up with science, and making
it improving to the mind and all that. A good,
square, honest, old chap was Yung Ling, and I have
heard that after he quitted the juggling business,
he got to be president of one of those new-fashioned
insurance companies, that undertake to pay you
back at the end of five years all the money you pay
in premiums and about four times as much besides.
I suppose it was the experience he got in the
juggling business that made him so successful as
an insurance man. Yung Ling had a very handsome daughter, who used to act as his assistant.
She was a perfectly respectable girl, but she had a

temper, and when she took a dislike to a man there wasn't anything bad enough for him in her estimation. She was reckless, too, as to what she would do to get square with anybody who, according to her fancy, had not treated her well. The Sword Swallower, who was a Frenchman, and, naturally, didn't know how a woman ought to be treated, did something or other that exasperated Lucille, and she served him out in a way that made him wish he had never been born. I'll tell you about it some day, if you want to hear the story, but it's too long to tell just now.

" Lucille, the Juggler's daughter, you understand, used to dress in pink tights and spangles, and stand in striking attitudes alongside of Yung Ling's table, and hand him things when he wanted them. Then, too, she did the collecting business—gathering up watches, and handkerchiefs, and other things from the audience whenever her father wanted a watch to pound in a mortar, or a handkerchief to tear into shreds. You've seen these tricks no end of times, I make no doubt. But her best part was the clairvoyant racket, that she and her father used to do after the regular juggling was over. Folks said it was a genuine miracle the way that girl could read letters with her eyes shut, and tell what her

12

father held up at the other end of the room. It's
curious how that clairvoyant act always fetches the
public, for of all the tricks, it's to my mind the
shallowest and the easiest to see through.

" Being, as I said, a very pretty girl, and a well-
behaved one in the main, it was natural that she
should attract a good deal of attention, and should
rake in bouquets and bracelets by the dozen. Old
Yung Ling kept a close watch on her, and wouldn't
allow no nonsense on the part of any of her
admirers. So long as they wanted to make presents,
he hadn't any sort of objection; but when a young
man who had sent Lucille a bracelet, and saw her
wear it on the stage, tried to call on her after the
show was over, he never saw any one except her
father, and he wasn't a very satisfactory sight, as a
rule, he having a short and sharp way with young
men, which wasn't the sort of thing they were
clamouring for.

" There was living in Cincinnati at the time—for
this was when I had a museum at Cincinnati—a
young fellow who was crazy on the subject of
juggling. He studied and practised till he was
really a pretty fair sort of amachure, and he used to
give entertainments to Sunday schools and in aid of
charities, that were occasionally almost worth seeing.

Well, when Yung Ling came to my place, this young fellow—I don't exactly recall his name at this minute—made his acquaintance, which was easy enough, provided you would stand the necessary quantity of beer,—and used to spend a good deal of time with him talking over the art of juggling. Yung Ling took a great fancy to the young man— now I seem to remember that his name was Tompkins—and had a pretty good opinion of his juggling. 'I like his style,' the old man said to me. 'He's got the helements of a good Prestidigitator in 'im, and with a little hintelligent teachin', 'e'll do very well.'

"Tompkins was a chap who had a good bit of money, and was a perfectly respectable man. The fact is, he was so tremendous respectable that the girls as a rule didn't like him, and used to call him 'Miss Nancy,' though it always seemed to me that if a girl can't find anything worse to say about a man than that he is like Miss Nancy, or any other woman, it shows that girls haven't a very good opinion of their own sex. However, that ain't my concern. Tompkins being so tremendous respectable, and having money as well as juggling talent, old Yung Ling thought he had found just the right man for a son-in-law, and introduced him to Lucille.

You see, the old man was wanting to retire, and he thought that if he could find the right sort of son-in-law, who would carry on the business at the old stand, he could retire at once, and give his whole mind to the insurance racket.

" Tompkins fell dead in love with Lucille the first time he saw her, and while he didn't see his way clear to go into juggling as a profession, preferring to be an amachure, he was ready to marry Lucille the minute she would agree to it. But that wasn't what Lucille wanted. I never saw a girl so down on a man as she was on poor Tompkins. Nothing that he could do pleased her, and she wouldn't give him a civil word, except when her father was at hand, and she was afraid the old man might scold her if she treated his young friend too cantankerously. She even refused to wear a bracelet that he gave her, and though of course she took it, as it was a middling valuable one, she told me that she should sell it the very first time she could get seventy-five per cent. of its value. She had a head for business, that girl, and nobody could accuse her of fooling away any chances that had money in them.

" Whether it was that Tompkins didn't have sense enough to see things clearly, or whether he was blinded by being in love, I can't pretend to say;

but he never seemed to know that the girl hated him, and he used to hang around her as if he supposed that she was glad to see him. He had a great desire to appear in my museum as a Juggler for one evening. Of course, he intended to be disguised, so that none of his acquaintances could recognise him ; but he said that unless he appeared at a regular entertainment like a regular professional, · he should never feel entire confidence in himself. Old Yung Ling was so anxious to have him succeed as a Juggler, that he agreed to give up one of his nights for nothing, provided he could arrange the matter with me ; and then Yung Ling came to me and said that I must charge the young man twenty-five dollars for the privilege of appearing on my stage, and that I could hand over fifteen dollars to him, and say nothing about it. I was always ready to accommodate anybody when I could conscientiously do so, and when Tompkins came to me with his proposal, I took his twenty-five dollars, and told him that he could take Yung Ling's place the next night, and that I would announce that, owing to Yung Ling's illness, I had engaged for one night only, at a vast expense, the only genuine Turkish Juggler then before the public.

" When Lucille found that she was expected to

act as an assistant to Tompkins, you may be sure
that she didn't like it, and there was something of
a row between her and the old man. However,
she was afraid of him, and always did as he said,
whether she liked it or not ; so, when evening came,
she was on hand as usual, looking, if anything,
prettier than ever. Somehow, I expected there
would be fun before the evening was over, so as
soon as it was time for the Juggler to take his turn,
I put one of my men in the ticket-office, and went
in to see how Tompkins would take with the public.

" He did look nervous, there was no denying that ;
but, then, every amachure who makes his first
appearance on a regular stage always is nervous,
no matter how well used he may be to performing
in drawing-rooms and for charitable objects. People
will overlook a good many mistakes in an amachure,
but when they pay their money to see a professional,
they expect that professional to come up to the
mark every time, and if he don't, why, there is apt
to be daybreak to westward. Nervousness on the
stage ain't of much consequence in the legitimate
drama, for there is always a prompter on hand to
pull an actor through if he forgets his lines ; and
then his lines are generally such rubbish that it
don't make much difference where he begins or

where he ends them. I once saw a Hamlet who played the part for the first time, he having pre-viously been captain of supernumeraries, and he was so frightened that, instead of giving the regu-lation speech to his father's ghost, he gave the speech that Macbeth makes to the ghost of Banquo. But there wasn't a man in the house who seemed to notice that anything was wrong. So far as the audience was concerned, as long as there was a ghost, it didn't matter to them whose ghost it was. Now, in the juggling business things are very different. A Juggler has to keep perfectly cool, for if he doesn't, he is sure to make a mistake, and when he makes a mistake, it spoils everything.

"Tompkins got along middling well with the first part of his programme, for it consisted of easy tricks with cards, things which any man can do who isn't positively shaking with fright. But pre-sently he comes to that good old trick of making an omelette in a man's hat. Lucille went down among the audience and borrowed a hat of one of our Common Councilmen, who had won a prize fight which brought him in nearly ten thousand dollars, and who hadn't drawn a sober breath for pretty near six weeks.

"Tompkins made his omelette all right, but he

didn't notice that when Lucille handed him the hat
to make it in, she had handed him the Common
Councilman's hat instead of the property hat which
ought to have been substituted for it. Barring this
mistake, he did the trick fairly well, and when it
was finished and he had given the omelette to a boy
in the audience, who stood ready, like all boys, to
eat anything that anybody might give him, he
thanked the owner of the hat, and sent it back to
him by Lucille. The moment the man saw the
hat, he said to Lucille: ' Look a here, my girl,
thishyer ain't no hat of mine '. Lucille, however,
didn't pay any attention to him, but tripped back
to the stage, and the man began to get pretty mad.
He rose up, and remarked, in a loud voice, that
any ' dashed Chinese Turk that thought he could
play off last year's hat on him had made a big
mistake, and that if he didn't get his own hat back
inside of two minutes there would be a change in
the programme that might be unhealthy '. By this
time Tompkins had found out his mistake, and was
beginning to grow pale, for he knew the Common
Councilman's reputation, and he knew that if it
came to a fight he was as good as done for. So he
calls out to the man and invites him to step on the
stage for one minute. The man came up, and

Tompkins whispered to him that he was going to play a new trick with the hat which had never before been seen in this country, and that he would place twenty-five dollars in his hands then and there, as a guarantee that his hat would be returned to him in good order. This satisfied the fellow for the moment, and he said he didn't want no guarantee, but that if he didn't get his hat back before the show was over, the Juggler's head would be so swelled up, that hats wouldn't be of any further use to him.

" If Tompkins was frightened before this accident occurred, it was nothing to his fright after it was over. I had half a mind to send word to him to faint away, and so bring his performance to a close ; but, then, I'm not fond of meddling, especially when it spoils fun. The next two or three tricks went off passably well, though when Tompkins tried to throw a ball up into the air, intending it should never come down again—which, of course, it couldn't when it was once hid up his sleeve—he accidentally let go of the ball, and it went up to the ceiling, and then came down and hit a woman on the side of the head, and led to her using such language that I had to interfere and put her out, for language is something that I never allow nobody to use inside of my show under any circumstances.

" You know the old trick where the Juggler pounds a man's watch to pieces in a mortar and then gives it back to him in good condition? Well, the time came for Tompkins to perform this trick, which is one of the very easiest of the whole list, and he began to look more cheerful as he reflected that there couldn't very well be

" HIT A WOMAN ON THE SIDE OF THE HEAD."

any mistake about this.

" But he didn't seem to remember that Lucille was assisting him, which made a heap of difference. She went down and borrowed a watch when the Juggler called for one, and she deliberately borrowed it of the Common Councilman, who told her as he gave it to her that any man who meant to do any damage to that watch, had better get into his grave and lie there comfortable before taking the watch in his hands. Lucille just smiled, and said that she guessed it would be all right, and then carried the watch back to Tompkins.

" The girl wasn't a bad Prestidigitator herself,

and if it hadn't been for old Yung Ling's prejudices
—for he was dead against the emancipation of
women—he might have trained her to be his suc-
cessor. It was her duty to change the watch of
the Common Councilman for the property watch,
but she managed not to do it, and the watch she
passed to Tompkins to put in the mortar was the
genuine one she had borrowed. It was a mighty
handsome watch, and had been presented to the
Councilman by his constituents in gratitude for
his efforts in procuring the repeal of the law for-
bidding the sale of liquor on Sundays. It was
engraved with his name, and was said to be worth
two hundred dollars, and I don't doubt it. Tompkins puts this watch in the mortar, and pounds it
into fine pieces, and then he draws out the property
watch, which was worth about ten cents, and,
saying that the gentleman would find that his watch
was uninjured, sent it back to him by Lucille.

" The Common Councilman looked at the watch,
and then he took and threw it at Tompkins' head
without saying a word. It didn't hit Tompkins,
but I am glad to say that it did hit Lucille in the
eye, for she deserved it, and it gave her a beautiful
black eye for the next week. Then the Councilman
rose up, took off his coat, and remarked ' Whoop ! '

at the top of his lungs. I stepped out for a policeman, for I knew the Councilman meant business,
and that I wasn't any sort of match for him.

"When I got back with the policeman, which

"THREW THE WATCH AT TOMPKINS' HEAD."

wasn't more than a minute, I found Tompkins
lying insensible on the stage, and the Councilman
dancing on him and inviting all the rest of the
world to come on. Nobody came on but the police-

man, and he came off quicker than he came on. I
never saw a man so completely knocked out in one
round as that policeman was. This time I went
out and got a squad of police, and after one of the
prettiest fights you ever dreamed of, the Councilman was ironed and carried off to a police magis-
trate, who apologised to him, and sent him home
in a carriage.

"Tompkins came to after a while, and went
home feeling about as small, and about as
sore, and about as sick of juggling as a man ever
felt. I will say for him that when the Common
Councilman sued me for the value of the watch
and hat, and for consequential damages, making
the whole bill a matter of five hundred dollars,
Tompkins came forward and paid it like a man.
But he seemed to have grown tired both of the
profession and of Lucille. He gave up coming to
see Yung Ling, and before the winter was over he
moved to St. Louis and went into business there,
which shows that he must have been pretty well
sick of life in general. That was the first and last
time I ever had an amachure Juggler in my show,
but I have always felt that I got enough amusement out of it to console me for the irregularity of
admitting an amachure on my stage."

CHAPTER XII.

THE BEARDED WOMAN.

"As I've said to you before," remarked the door-keeper, "falling in love is mainly a matter of a man's height. The taller you are the more likely you are to fall in love, and if you are particularly tall you are bound to have it bad. Now, who ever heard of a Dwarf being in love with anything except him-self? I've known some fifteen or sixteen regular pro-fessional Dwarfs, besides a lot of amachure Dwarfs, and I never knew one who could care two straws for any human being—not even a dog. Whereas, the moment a man gets to be seven or eight feet high, he is ready to fall in love with pretty near every woman he meets. I once knew a Giant who broke his heart over a woman—and she was a Bearded Woman at that. The man died, sir, of a broken heart, just as you or I might die of a broken neck. If he'd been a resonable height, say five feet ten, which I take it is about your height, he would have lived through his trouble, and probably married

(178)

some other woman. Being a Giant is an easy way
of earning a living, provided, of course, you're lazy.
Next to being what they call in Europe 'a constitutional king,' it's about the softest berth a man can
have. All the same it has its disadvantages, and so
far as I am concerned I never want to be over five feet
ten. A middling-sized man can enjoy life, and take
his troubles easy when they do come. It's the six
and seven footers who know what real heartache is,
judging from what I have seen in the course of a
pretty long life.

"Thishyer Giant, the one that died of a broken
heart, travelled with me about fifteen years ago,
when I was on the road, and before I settled down
to keeping a permanent museum. His name was
Tom Brixton, and he was an Englishman. He
was a good seven feet three inches in height, and
when he got his professional boots and helmet on
he was not to be beat by any Giant in the business.
His professional name I forget, but he was always
billed as the Afghanistan Giant, and wore a uniform
which was supposed to be the uniform of an Afghanistan Colonel. A mighty handsome uniform it was
too, and I designed it myself. It consisted of a
yellow dress coat, with black facings and scarlet
trousers. The helmet was a dark blue, and the

boots, which came half-way up the leg, were white leather, glazed, and embroidered with gold. I won't go so far as to say to you that it was the regular uniform of the Thirty-Fifth Afghanistan Light Infantry, as the bills said it was, but it was about as swell a uniform as you will ever see, outside of a volunteer regiment in a Montana town.

"Tom was not very strong in the head, which, as I have told you, is a characteristic of Giants. What ought to make brains in them seems to go to making bone, and the consequence is that they haven't their share of intelligence, as a general thing. Did you ever think what would have been the consequence if Napoleon had been six feet two inches high? Why, sir, he wouldn't have had sense enough to command a corporal's guard. A man can't run to leg and brain at the same time, and nobody knows that better than soldiers. That's why our men, at the beginning of the Civil War, had so much faith in General McClellan. It was because he was a short, dumpy man. That's why the British soldiers have such a tremenjous opinion of Lord Roberts, who, from all I read, is a first-class general. Lord Roberts is another of your small men, and that accounts for the splendid way in

which he got his men out of Afghanistan. You
see I do know something about Afghanistan, even
if I don't happen to be familiar with the uniforms
of the Afghanistan regular army.

"Admitting that Tom Brixton didn't have quite
his fair share of sense, that was all you could say
against him. He was sober, kind-hearted, and as
honest as the day is long. You would never catch
him shirking his morning dumb-bells as most Giants
will do if you don't watch them, and then, of course,
they get round-shouldered, which lessens their
height and diminishes their value. But Tom knew
what is an honest Giant's duty to his employers, and
he never failed to do everything in his power to keep
his height up to the highest figure. Then again, if
anybody was in trouble they always went straight
to the Giant for sympathy. He was for ever giving
this man or that man good advice, and lending him
money, and as for the women, they all said he was
just the dearest old chap that ever was born. Not
that he was really old, you understand, for I don't
think he could have been over forty, but his moral
character was so good that it gave him the general
effect of being an old man. Anyway, he wasn't too
old to have given up falling in love, for all the time
he was with me he was more or less sweet on some

13

woman or another—it didn't seem to matter so very
much who she was.

"We were showing in St. Louis when I made an
engagement with a Bearded Woman. Contrary to
public opinion the Bearded Woman is always
genuine. I don't exactly understand why this is,
for there is nothing that is so easy to imitate
as a Bearded Woman. However, it has got to
be a point of honour with managers never to play
off an imitation Bearded Woman on the public, and
whenever you see one you can make up your mind
that she is a sure enough woman with a genuine
beard. The fact is Bearded Women are middling
easy to produce. I know half a dozen women my-
sélf, who, with a little care and cultivation, could
raise beards that would give then a steady and comfortable income. But then women as a rule have
very little business enterprise.

"Thishyer Bearded Woman was about twenty-five
years old, and she would have been a very handsome girl if it had not been for her beard and mous-
tache. Her beard was jet black, and about five inches
long, and it was thick and glossy, and black enough
for a first-class professional gambler. She was a
nice girl, too, was Mamselle—I don't just remember
at this minute what her professional name was, ex-

cept that it was French, though the girl herself came from Indiana. Mamselle was a thorough lady in her ways, and I engaged her without inquiring too much about her relations, which is always risky, for if a freak has a mother, and a lot of sisters and brothers, they will be hanging around the museum half the time, and giving you a lot of trouble. I afterwards found that the girl hadn't a relation in the world, and not a cent except what she made by exhibiting herself. Perhaps it was being so alone in the world that made her grateful to the Giant for his sympathy.

"Of course he was dead in love with her before she had been in the show two days. He took a sort of charge of her the very day she arrived, and introduced her to the other members of the company, and explained the rules and customs of the place, and made himself generally useful. It wasn't long before it was clear to everybody that the Bearded Woman was very fond of Tom, and about the fourth week of her engagement Tom came to me and said he wanted my permission to get married. You see it is always put in the contract that no freak is to marry without the manager's consent. This is necessary; otherwise you couldn't possibly enforce discipline, and keep your people from going into the

street, and so making themselves cheap and value-
less—and other nonsense of that sort.

"I told Tom that marrying was stark nonsense

"OF COURSE HE WAS DEAD IN LOVE WITH HER."

for him. 'You're getting fifty dollars a week now,'
said I, 'and Mamselle is getting thirty. Fifty and
thirty is eighty. Now, if you marry her you'll only

be getting forty dollars a-piece, and you'll have to spend a lot of money in supporting her if she takes a notion to abandon public life, and looks to you, as her husband, for support.'

" ' But I can't live without her, Colonel,' said the Giant. ' You've no idea how I love that woman.'

" ' Oh, yes, I have,' said I ; ' I've seen you in just the same state half a dozen times, and you always come out of it all right. I won't say I'll refuse to give you permission to get married if you stick to the notion, for I don't mind admitting that you've earned a good deal of consideration from me by your conduct since you came here, which has been square and level-headed, but I want you to wait a while yet before you actually do marry. Wait a month, and then come to me and we'll see what can be done.'

" Tom agreed to this, and I took the first opportunity of talking to Mamselle about the matter, hoping that she would be more reasonable than the Giant, seeing as she wasn't much more than half his height. But she was worse if anything. ' I love him,' said she, ' and I am going to marry him if he wants me to.'

" ' What on earth do you want to do that for,'

I asked her, 'when you are independent and earning a good thirty dollars a week?'

" 'There's other things in the world besides salary,' replied she. 'Colonel, I'm twenty-nine years old (she had always said twenty-five before)

"IF YOU ONLY KNEW HOW ASHAMED I AM OF IT!"

and Tom is the first man that ever dreamed of marrying me. You know well enough that a Bearded Woman can find plenty of men to stare at her, but there ain't one of them that don't think she is a disgusting sight. If you only knew how I hate that horrible beard, and how ashamed I am of it! With-

out it I'd be a handsome woman, and now I'm so
ugly that I make a show of myself. How do you
suppose I like to spend my life alone, without a
lover, or a husband, or children, or a home, like
other women ? Do you know I was never kissed
in all my life till Tom kissed me! And you want
me to throw away the only chance of happiness that
ever came to me. Colonel! I'd marry Tom if I
knew that I'd die the next hour.'

" ' Marry him you shall, my dear,' said I ; for
now that she had explained things I hadn't the
heart to disappoint the poor woman, and I saw for
the first time how a woman may be in the very
front rank of her profession and yet be unhappy.
' Your engagement will be up in three weeks, and
then I'll give you a wedding myself, and renew the
contract for fifty dollars a week instead of thirty.'
Having said this, I left her pretty sudden, for when
I give way to a fit of generosity it is apt to carry
me altogether too far.

" They were married in the museum, no one
being present except the company and the employees,
and that evening, an hour after the show was over,
Tom took his wife to a little house he had rented
not far from our place. He told me that while he
was very grateful to me for my offer, his wife didn't

intend to appear before the public any more. She was going to keep house, which is what every woman freak that was ever born is always longing to do, and he calculated to drive to his house in a closed cab every night, after the street was deserted.

" ' You know, I suppose,' said I to him, ' that fifty dollars a week is equal to ten per cent. on twenty thousand dollars. Your wife's beard is worth twenty thousand dollars, and you are foolish enough to let a sum like that lie idle ! Tom, I'm really astonished at you.'

" ' She isn't going to have a beard much longer,' replied the Giant. ' There is a doctor who has discovered a new way of removing beards, and he says he can do it so that it will never come back, and nobody will ever imagine that Emma ever had such a thing.'

" ' This is worse and worse,' said I. ' Now you are proposing to destroy twenty thousand dollars of paying capital. I consider such things positively wicked, let alone the awful foolishness of them. Just you listen to reason, and make your wife keep her beard and go on the stage again as soon as she gets tired of keeping house, as all women will, after they have tried it a while. A beard like hers is a

gift of Providence, and it's nothing less than in-
gratitude to throw it away.'

" ' I can't help that,' said Tom. ' My wife wants
to be like other women, and she shall be, if I can
bring it about. What's twenty thousand dollars
compared with making her life happy ? '

" Tom was a regular Giant, you see ; no common
sense, and very little of any other kind. But after
all I had said, I considered that I had done my
duty, and that it wasn't my place to meddle any
more, even if Tom should want to get a surgeon
to cut him down to an ordinary height. So I said
no more, and took the Bearded Woman's name off
the bills, and looked around for some attraction to
take her place.

" One day, about a fortnight after the conversation
I had with him, Tom didn't come to the museum in
the morning, and sent a note saying that his wife
was very sick, and he couldn't leave her. I meant
to go down in the course of the evening and see how
the woman was, but about eight o'clock a messenger
came for me and said that Tom's wife was dying,
and that he wanted to see me. I lost no time in
getting to his house. The messenger went with
me, and showed me up into the bedroom. It was
a little bit of a room, hardly six by twelve feet.

Tom's wife was lying in bed, and Tom was kneeling beside her, with his legs doubled up in all sorts of ways, for there wasn't room for them between the bed and the wall. There was a priest there—for the woman was a Roman Catholic—and he had just finished his part of the proceedings and was going away as I came in.

"'What's the matter?' I whispered to Tom. 'Is it anything serious?' Though I knew well enough that if it wasn't serious the priest wouldn't have been there.

"'The doctor says she can't possibly live till morning,' replied Tom. 'It's erysipelas. She don't know me now, and she never will again. Look at her face and you'll see what is the matter.'

"I took the candle and looked at the poor woman. All her beard was gone, but in the place of it was a horrible fiery swelling that looked just as if she had been burned with a hot iron.

"'It's what the doctor did who removed the beard,' said Tom. 'The last thing she said to me, half an hour ago, before she went out of her head, was: "Never mind, dear. The beard is gone, and in the next world I shall be like other women, and you can be proud of me." As if I shouldn't be proud of her, no matter how she might look.'

" Well, not to dwell on a painful subject, the poor
woman died that night, soon after I had gone home.
I sent the Tattooed Girl down to the house to help
Tom, for she was a good sort of girl, and had
always been very friendly with the deceased, and I
gave Tom's wife a bang-up funeral that would have
pleased the most fashionable corpse in Chicago.

" After the funeral was over, I tried my best to
comfort Tom.   He had gone to the cemetery in a
cab, and had stood by the grave, never caring a rap
for all the people who saw him gratis, and never
seeming to reflect that he was permanently lowering
his market value.   The fact is he was all broke up.
I said to him :—

" ' It's all over now, my boy, and you must try
to bear up and forget about it.   We've all got to die
sometime, and if we don't die first, our friends will.
Your wife was a good woman, and I make no doubt
she's having a first-class time in Heaven, and you
want to get over mourning for her, and begin to
enjoy life again as soon as possible.'

" ' Thank you kindly, Colonel,' says the Giant,
' but I guess we'd better not talk about it just now.'

" ' Well,' says I, ' just you take a vacation, and
go to New York, or some other place, for a change
of scene, being careful, of course, not to exhibit

yourself gratis. I'll continue your salary, and, b'gosh, you can take two weeks, if you want to.'

"You see, I was so blamed sorry for the chap that my feelings were beginning to get the better of my judgment.

"'You are as kind as they make 'em,' replied Tom, 'and I expect to take a mighty big vacation before long, but not just yet.'

"This happened on a Monday. Tom came to the show as usual the day after the funeral, but the next day he wrote that he wasn't feeling quite up to it, and would stay away for a few days. The next Sunday night, he sent for me, and there he was, lying in the bed that his wife died in, and looking like a ghost. There was a doctor standing by the bed, and when I asked Tom what was the matter, and he answered, 'It is just death, that's all,' I glanced at the doctor, and the man nodded.

"'I'm going to see her,' said the Giant, 'and I'm happier than I ever expected to be again. If you've any message, Colonel, I'll take it. You always was a good friend to her, and she was pretty fond of you.'

"'You can't really mean that you're going to die?' exclaimed I. 'Why, what in the world has

come to you?   Have you had an accident, or anything of that kind?'

"'There ain't nothing the matter with me,' said
Tom, 'except that I've got through living.   I

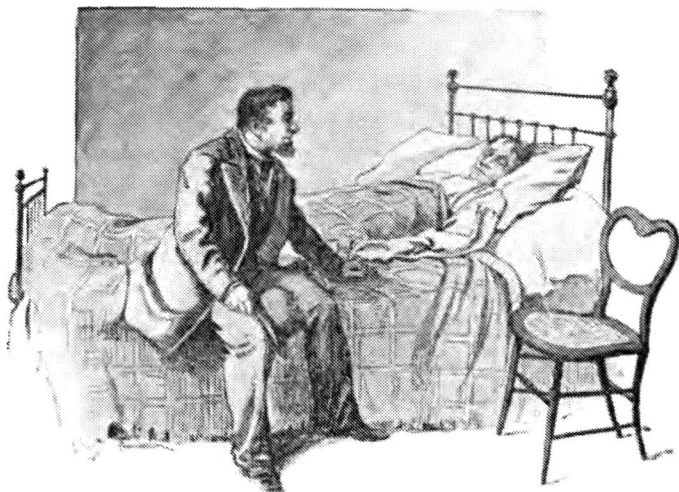

"' I'M GOING TO SEE HER,' SAID THE GIANT."

wanted to say good-bye to you, and thank you for
your kindness.   Here's the priest coming in, so
you'll have to go.'

"'I didn't know you were a Roman Catholic,'
said I.   It was a stupid thing to say at such a

time, but I was regularly rattled, and hardly knew what I said.

"'I don't know the difference between one religion and another,' Tom answered; 'but thishyer was her religion, and what was hers is mine.'

"The doctor and I went into the next room, and the priest came in and attended to his duties. It took a good while, and when the priest went away, and the doctor and I went back into the room, Tom was lying, looking mighty weak, but very happy. Even while we were looking at him he closed his eyes, and I thought he had dropped off to sleep, but the doctor felt his pulse, and then put his hand over his heart, and said, 'It's all over'.

"Afterwards the doctor told me that Tom died of failure of the heart.

"His heart may have failed, but it was because it was broke. If ever a man died of broken heart it was that identical Giant. When you come to think of a man breaking his heart over a woman with a beard, it does seem sort of impossible, but it's the gospel truth I've been giving you. Tom left all his money to me; he having no relations that he knew of. There was five hundred and fifty dollars of it, and I spent every cent of it on his funeral and his tombstone. You can see the stone any day in the

Lake Cemetery. The same stone does for both him and his wife, and the inscription says 'that they were beautiful in their lives, and in death were not divided'. That statement is a little steep perhaps, but if you're going to tell the cold truth on tomb-stones, men might as well be born without any imagination at all."

ABERDEEN UNIVERSITY PRESS.

MESSRS. LONGMANS, GREEN, & CO.'S
CLASSIFIED CATALOGUE
OF
WORKS IN GENERAL LITERATURE.

History, Politics, Polity, Political Memoirs, &c.

Abbott.—A HISTORY OF GREECE. By EVELYN ABBOTT, M.A., LL.D.
Part I.—From the Earliest Times to the Ionian Revolt. Crown 8vo., 10s. 6d.
Part II.—500-445 B.C. Cr. 8vo., 10s. 6d.

Acland and Ransome.—A HANDBOOK IN OUTLINE OF THE POLITICAL HISTORY OF ENGLAND TO 1894. Chronologically Arranged. By A. H. DYKE ACLAND, M.P., and CYRIL RANSOME, M.A. Cr. 8vo., 6s.

ANNUAL REGISTER (THE). A Review of Public Events at Home and Abroad, for the year 1894. 8vo., 18s.
Volumes of the ANNUAL REGISTER for the years 1863-1893 can still be had. 18s. each.

Armstrong.—ELIZABETH FARNESE; The Termagant of Spain. By EDWARD ARMSTRONG, M.A. 8vo., 16s.

Arnold.—Works by T. ARNOLD, D.D., formerly Head Master of Rugby School.
INTRODUCTORY LECTURES ON MODERN HISTORY. 8vo., 7s. 6d.
MISCELLANEOUS WORKS. 8vo., 7s. 6d.

Bagwell.—IRELAND UNDER THE TUDORS. By RICHARD BAGWELL, LL.D. 3 vols. Vols. I. and II. From the first Invasion of the Northmen to the year 1578. 8vo., 32s. Vol. III. 1578-1603. 8vo., 18s.

Ball.—HISTORICAL REVIEW OF THE LEGISLATIVE SYSTEMS OPERATIVE IN IRELAND, from the Invasion of Henry the Second to the Union (1172-1800). By the Rt. Hon. J. T. BALL. 8vo., 6s.

Besant.—THE HISTORY OF LONDON. By WALTER BESANT. With 74 Illustrations. Crown 8vo., 1s. 9d. Or bound as a School Prize Book, 2s. 6d.

Brassey.—PAPERS AND ADDRESSES. By LORD BRASSEY.
NAVAL AND MARITIME, 1872-1893. 2 vols. Crown 8vo., 10s.
MERCANTILE MARINE AND NAVIGATION, 1871-1894. Crown 8vo., 5s.
POLITICAL AND MISCELLANEOUS, 1861-1894. Crown 8vo., 5s.

Bright.—A HISTORY OF ENGLAND. By the Rev. J. FRANCK BRIGHT, D.D.,
Period I. MEDIÆVAL MONARCHY: A.D. 449 to 1485. Crown 8vo., 4s. 6d.
Period II. PERSONAL MONARCHY: 1485 to 1688. Crown 8vo., 5s.
Period III. CONSTITUTIONAL MONARCHY: 1689 to 1837. Cr. 8vo., 7s. 6d.
Period IV. THE GROWTH OF DEMOCRACY: 1837 to 1880. Cr. 8vo., 6s.

Buckle.—HISTORY OF CIVILISATION IN ENGLAND AND FRANCE, SPAIN AND SCOTLAND. By HENRY THOMAS BUCKLE. 3 vols. Crown 8vo., 24s.

Burke.—A HISTORY OF SPAIN, from the Earliest Times to the Death of Ferdinand the Catholic. By ULICK RALPH BURKE, M.A. 2 vols. 8vo., 32s.

Chesney.—INDIAN POLITY: a View of the System of Administration in India. By General Sir GEORGE CHESNEY, K.C.B., M.P. With Map showing all the Administrative Divisions of British India. 8vo. 21s.

Creighton.—HISTORY OF THE PAPACY DURING THE REFORMATION. By MANDELL CREIGHTON, D.D., LL.D., Bishop of Peterborough. Vols. I. and II., 1378-1464, 32s. Vols. III. and IV., 1464-1518., 24s. Vol. V., 1517-1527. 8vo., 15s.

Cuningham.—A SCHEME FOR IMPERIAL FEDERATION: a Senate for the Empire. By GRANVILLE C. CUNINGHAM, of Montreal, Canada. Cr. 8vo., 3s. 6d.

Curzon.—PERSIA AND THE PERSIAN QUESTION. By the HON. GEORGE N. CURZON, M.P. With 9 Maps, 96 Illustrations, Appendices, and an Index. 2 vols. 8vo., 42s.

History, Politics, Polity, Political Memoirs, &c.—*continued.*

De Tocqueville. — DEMOCRACY IN AMERICA. By ALEXIS DE TOCQUEVILLE. 2 vols. Crown 8vo., 16s.

Dickinson.—THE DEVELOPMENT OF PARLIAMENT DURING THE NINETEENTH CENTURY. By G. LOWES DICKINSON, M.A. 8vo. 7s. 6d.

Ewald.—THE HISTORY OF ISRAEL. By HEINRICH EWALD, Professor in the University of Göttingen. 8 vols. 8vo., Vols. I. and II., 24s. Vols. III. and IV., 21s. Vol. V., 18s. Vol. VI., 16s. Vol. VII., 21s. Vol. VIII., 18s.

Fitzpatrick.—SECRET SERVICE UNDER PITT. By W. J. FITZPATRICK, F.S.A., Author of ' Correspondence of Daniel O'Connell'. 8vo., 7s. 6d.

Froude.—Works by JAMES A. FROUDE.
THE HISTORY OF ENGLAND, from the Fall of Wolsey to the Defeat of the Spanish Armada. 12 vols. Cr. 8vo., 3s. 6d. each.
THE ENGLISH IN IRELAND IN THE EIGHTEENTH CENTURY.
Cabinet Edition. 3 vols. Cr. 8vo., 18s.
Silver Library Edition. 3 vols. Cr. 8vo., 10s. 6d.
SHORT STUDIES ON GREAT SUBJECTS. 4 vols. Cr. 8vo., 3s. 6d. each.
THE DIVORCE OF CATHERINE OF ARAGON. Crown 8vo., 6s.
THE SPANISH STORY OF THE ARMADA, and other Essays. Cr. 8vo., 3s. 6d.
LECTURES ON THE COUNCIL OF TRENT. 8vo., 12s. 6d.
ENGLISH SEAMEN IN THE SIXTEENTH CENTURY. Crown 8vo., 6s.
CÆSAR: a Sketch. Cr. 8vo., 3s. 6d.

Gardiner.—Works by SAMUEL RAWSON GARDINER, D.C.L., LL.D.
HISTORY OF ENGLAND, from the Accession of James I. to the Outbreak of the Civil War, 1603-1642. 10 vols. Crown 8vo., 6s. each.
HISTORY OF THE GREAT CIVIL WAR, 1642-1649. 4 vols. Cr. 8vo., 6s. each.
HISTORY OF THE COMMONWEALTH AND THE PROTECTORATE, 1649-1660. Vol. I., 1649-1651. With 14 Maps. 8vo., 21s.
THE STUDENT'S HISTORY OF ENGLAND, With 378 Illustrations. Cr. 8vo., 12s.
Also in Three Volumes, price 4s. each.

Greville.—A JOURNAL OF THE REIGNS OF KING GEORGE IV., KING WILLIAM IV., AND QUEEN VICTORIA. By CHARLES C. F. GREVILLE, 8 vols. Crown 8vo., 6s. each.

Hearn.—THE GOVERNMENT OF ENGLAND: its Structure and its Development By W. EDWARD HEARN. 8vo., 16s.

Herbert.—THE DEFENCE OF PLEVNA, 1877. Written by One who took Part in it. By WILLIAM V. HERBERT. With Maps. 8vo., 18s.

Historic Towns.—Edited by E. A. FREEMAN, D.C.L., and Rev. WILLIAM HUNT, M.A. With Maps and Plans. Crown 8vo., 3s. 6d. each.

Bristol. By the Rev. W. Hunt.	London. By Rev. W. J. Loftie.
Carlisle. By Mandell Creighton, D.D., Bishop of Peterborough.	Oxford. By Rev. C. W. Boase.
	Winchester. By Rev. G.W. Kitchin, D.D.,
Cinque Ports. By Montagu Burrows.	York. By Rev. James Raine.
Colchester. By Rev. E. L. Cutts.	New York. By Theodore Roosevelt.
Exeter. By E. A. Freeman.	Boston (U.S.). By Henry Cabot Lodge.

Joyce.—A SHORT HISTORY OF IRELAND, from the Earliest Times to 1608. By P. W. JOYCE, LL.D. Cr. 8vo., 10s. 6d.

Kaye and Malleson.—Works by.
HISTORY OF THE SEPOY WAR IN INDIA. 1857-1858. By Sir JOHN W. KAYE, K.C.S.I., F.R.S. 3 vols. 8vo. Vol. I. 18s. : Vol. II. 20s. : Vol. III. 20s.
HISTORY OF THE INDIAN MUTINY, 1857-1858. Commencing from the close of the Second Volume of Sir John W. Kaye's ' History of the Sepoy War.' By Colonel G. B. MALLESON, C.S.I. 3 vols. 8vo. Vol. I., with Map, 20s. ; Vol. II., with 4 Maps and Plans, 20s.; Vol. III., with 4 Maps, 20s.
ANALYTICAL INDEX TO SIR JOHN W. KAYE'S ' HISTORY OF THE SEPOY WAR ' AND COL. G. B. MALLESON'S ' HISTORY OF THE INDIAN MUTINY,' (Combined in one volume.) By FREDERIC PINCOTT. 8vo., 10s. 6d.
KAYE AND MALLESON'S ' HISTORY OF THE INDIAN MUTINY, 1857-1858.' (Being a Cabinet Edition of the above Works.) Edited by Colonel G. B. MALLESON. With Analytical Index by FREDERIC PINCOTT, and Maps and Plans. 6 vols. Cr. 8vo., 6s. each.

Knight.—MADAGASCAR IN WAR TIME: the Experiences of *The Times* Special Correspondent with the Hovas during the French Invasion of 1895. By E. F. KNIGHT. With numerous Illustrations and Map. 8vo., 12s. 6d.

Lang.—ST. ANDREWS. By ANDREW LANG. With 8 Plates and 24 Illustrations in the Text, by T. HODGE. 8vo., 15s. net.

History, Politics, Polity, Political Memoirs, &c.—*continued.*

Lecky.—Works by WILLIAM EDWARD HARTPOLE LECKY.

HISTORY OF ENGLAND IN THE EIGHTEENTH CENTURY.
Library Edition. 8 vols. 8vo., £7 4s.
Cabinet Edition. ENGLAND. 7 vols. Cr. 8vo., 6s. each. IRELAND. 5 vols. Crown 8vo., 6s. each.
HISTORY OF EUROPEAN MORALS FROM AUGUSTUS TO CHARLEMAGNE. 2 vols. Crown 8vo., 16s.
HISTORY OF THE RISE AND INFLUENCE OF THE SPIRIT OF RATIONALISM IN EUROPE. 2 vols. Crown 8vo., 16s.
DEMOCRACY AND LIBERTY. 2 vols. 8vo., 36s.
THE EMPIRE : its Value and its Growth. An Address delivered at the Imperial Institute. Crown 8vo., 1s. 6d.

Macaulay.—Works by LORD MACAULAY.
COMPLETE WORKS.
Cabinet Ed. 16 vols. Post 8vo., £4 16s.
Library Edition. 8 vols. 8vo., £5 5s.
HISTORY OF ENGLAND FROM THE ACCESSION OF JAMES THE SECOND.
Popular Edition. 2 vols. Cr. 8vo., 5s.
Student's Edit. 2 vols. Cr. 8vo., 12s.
People's Edition. 4 vols. Cr. 8vo., 16s.
Cabinet Edition. 8 vols. Post 8vo., 48s.
Library Edition. 5 vols. 8vo., £4.
CRITICAL AND HISTORICAL ESSAYS, WITH LAYS OF ANCIENT ROME, in 1 volume.
Popular Edition. Crown 8vo., 2s. 6d.
Authorised Edition. Crown 8vo., 2s. 6d., or 3s. 6d., gilt edges.
Silver Library Edition. Crown 8vo., 3s. 6d.
CRITICAL AND HISTORICAL ESSAYS.
Student's Edition. 1 vol. Cr. 8vo., 6s.
People's Edition. 2 vols. Cr. 8vo., 8s.
Trevelyan Edit. 2 vols. Cr. 8vo., 9s.
Cabinet Edition. 4 vols. Post 8vo., 24s.
Library Edition. 3 vols. 8vo., 36s.
ESSAYS which may be had separately, price 6d. each sewed, 1s. each cloth.

Addison and Walpole.	Lord Clive.
Frederick the Great.	The Earl of Chatham(Two Essays).
Lord Bacon.	Ranke and Gladstone.
Croker's Boswell's Johnson.	Milton and Machiavelli.
Hallam's Constitutional History.	Lord Byron,and The Comic Dramatists of the Restoration.
Warren Hastings (3d. swd., 6d. cl.).	

Macaulay.—Works by LORD MACAULAY.—*continued.*
MISCELLANEOUS WRITINGS AND SPEECHES.
Popular Edition. Cr. 8vo., 2s. 6d.
Cabinet Edition. Including Indian Penal Code, Lays of Ancient Rome, and Miscellaneous Poems. 4 vols. Post 8vo., 24s.
SELECTIONS FROM THE WRITINGS OF LORD MACAULAY. Edited, with Occasional Notes, by the Right Hon. Sir G. O. Trevelyan, Bart. Crown 8vo., 6s.

Mackinnon.—THE UNION OF ENGLAND AND SCOTLAND: a Study of International History. By JAMES MACKINNON, Ph.D., Examiner in History to the University of Edinburgh. 8vo., 16s.

May.—THE CONSTITUTIONAL HISTORY OF ENGLAND since the Accession of George III. 1760-1870. By Sir THOMAS ERSKINE MAY, K.C.B. (Lord Farnborough). 3 vols. Crown 8vo., 18s.

Merivale.—Works by the Very Rev. CHARLES MERIVALE, late Dean of Ely.
HISTORY OF THE ROMANS UNDER THE EMPIRE.
Cabinet Edition. 8 vols. Cr. 8vo., 48s.
Silver Library Edition. 8 vols. Cr. 8vo., 3s. 6d. each.
THE FALL OF THE ROMAN REPUBLIC: a Short History of the Last Century of the Commonwealth. 12mo., 7s. 6d.

Montague.—THE ELEMENTS OF ENGLISH CONSTITUTIONAL HISTORY. By F. C. MONTAGUE, M.A. Cr. 8vo., 3s. 6d.

Richman.—APPENZELL : Pure Democracy and Pastoral Life in Inner-Rhoden. A Swiss Study. By IRVING B. RICHMAN, Consul-General of the United States to Switzerland. With Maps. Crown 8vo., 5s.

Seebohm.—Works by FREDERIC SEEBOHM.
THE ENGLISH VILLAGE COMMUNITY Examined in its Relations to the Manorial and Tribal Systems, &c. With 13 Maps and Plates. 8vo., 16s.
THE TRIBAL SYSTEM IN WALES: being Part of an Inquiry into the Structure and Methods of Tribal Society. With 3 Maps. 8vo., 12s.

History, Politics, Polity, Political Memoirs, &c.—*continued.*

Sharpe.—LONDON AND THE KINGDOM: a History derived mainly from the Archives at Guildhall in the custody of the Corporation of the City of London. By REGINALD R. SHARPE, D.C.L., Records Clerk in the Office of the Town Clerk of the City of London. 3 vols. 8vo. 10s. 6d. each.

Sheppard.—MEMORIALS OF ST. JAMES'S PALACE. By the Rev. EDGAR SHEPPARD, M.A., Sub-Dean of the Chapels Royal. With 41 full-page Plates (8 photo-intaglio), and 32 Illustrations in the Text. 2 Vols. 8vo, 36s. net.

Smith.—CARTHAGE AND THE CARTHAGINIANS. By R. BOSWORTH SMITH, M.A., Assistant Master in Harrow School. With Maps, Plans, &c. Cr. 8vo., 3s. 6d.

Stephens.—A HISTORY OF THE FRENCH REVOLUTION. By H. MORSE STEPHENS, Balliol College, Oxford. 3 vols. 8vo. Vols. I. and II., 18s. each.

Stubbs.—HISTORY OF THE UNIVERSITY OF DUBLIN, from its Foundation to the End of the Eighteenth Century. By J. W. STUBBS. 8vo., 12s. 6d.

Sutherland.—THE HISTORY OF AUSTRALIA AND NEW ZEALAND, from 1606 to 1890. By ALEXANDER SUTHERLAND, M.A., and GEORGE SUTHERLAND, M.A. Crown 8vo., 2s. 6d.

Todd.—PARLIAMENTARY GOVERNMENT IN THE BRITISH COLONIES. By ALPHEUS TODD, LL.D. 8vo., 30s. net.

Wakeman and Hassall.—ESSAYS INTRODUCTORY TO THE STUDY OF ENGLISH CONSTITUTIONAL HISTORY. Edited by HENRY OFFLEY WAKEMAN, M.A., and ARTHUR HASSALL, M.A. Crown 8vo., 6s.

Walpole.—Works by SPENCER WALPOLE.

HISTORY OF ENGLAND FROM THE CONCLUSION OF THE GREAT WAR IN 1815 TO 1858. 6 vols. Cr. 8vo., 6s. each.

THE LAND OF HOME RULE: being an Account of the History and Institutions of the Isle of Man. Cr. 8vo., 6s.

Wood-Martin.—PAGAN IRELAND: an Archæological Sketch. A Handbook of Irish Pre-Christian Antiquities. By W. G. WOOD-MARTIN, M.R.I.A. 412 Illustrations. 8vo., 15s.

Wylie.—HISTORY OF ENGLAND UNDER HENRY IV. By JAMES HAMILTON WYLIE, M.A., one of H. M. Inspectors of Schools. 3 vols. Crown 8vo. Vol. I., 1399-1404, 10s. 6d. Vol. II. 15s. Vol. III. 15s. [Vol. IV. *in the press.*

Biography, Personal Memoirs, &c.

Armstrong.—THE LIFE AND LETTERS OF EDMUND J. ARMSTRONG. Edited by G. F. ARMSTRONG. Fcp. 8vo., 7s. 6d.

Bacon.—LETTERS AND LIFE OF FRANCIS BACON, INCLUDING ALL HIS OCCASIONAL WORKS. Edited by J. SPEDDING. 7 vols. 8vo., £4 4s.

Bagehot.—BIOGRAPHICAL STUDIES. By WALTER BAGEHOT. Cr. 8vo., 3s. 6d.

Blackwell.—PIONEER WORK IN OPENING THE MEDICAL PROFESSION TO WOMEN: Autobiographical Sketches. By ELIZABETH BLACKWELL. Crown 8vo., 6s.

Boyd.—Works by A. K. H. BOYD, D.D., LL.D.

TWENTY-FIVE YEARS OF ST. ANDREWS. 1865-1890. 2 vols. 8vo. Vol. I., 12s. Vol. II., 15s.

ST. ANDREWS AND ELSEWHERE: Glimpses of Some Gone and of Things Left. 8vo., 15s.

THE LAST YEARS OF ST. ANDREWS: September 1890 to September 1895. 8vo., 15s.

Buss.—FRANCES MARY BUSS AND HER WORK FOR EDUCATION. By ANNIE E. RIDLEY. With 5 Portraits and 4 Illustrations. Crown 8vo., 7s. 6d.

Carlyle.—THOMAS CARLYLE: a History of his Life. By JAMES A. FROUDE. 1795-1835. 2 vols. Crown 8vo., 7s. 1834-1881. 2 vols. Crown 8vo., 7s.

Erasmus.—LIFE AND LETTERS OF ERASMUS. By JAMES A. FROUDE. Crown 8vo., 6s.

Fox.—THE EARLY HISTORY OF CHARLES JAMES FOX. By the Right Hon. Sir G. O. TREVELYAN, Bart., M.P.
Library Edition. 8vo., 18s.
Cabinet Edition. Crown 8vo., 6s.

Halford.—THE LIFE OF SIR HENRY HALFORD, Bart., G.C.H., M.D., F.R.S. By WILLIAM MUNK, M.D., F.S.A. 8vo, 12s. 6d.

Hamilton.—LIFE OF SIR WILLIAM HAMILTON. By R. P. GRAVES. 8vo. 3 vols. 15s. each.

Havelock.—MEMOIRS OF SIR HENRY HAVELOCK, K.C.B. By JOHN CLARK MARSHMAN. Crown 8vo., 3s. 6d.

Haweis.—Works by the Rev. H. R. HAWEIS, M.A.
MY MUSICAL LIFE. With Portrait of Richard Wagner and 3 Illustrations. Crown 8vo., 7s. 6d.
MUSIC AND MORALS. With Portrait of the Author, and numerous Illustrations, Facsimiles, and Diagrams. Cr. 8vo., 7s. 6d.

Biography, Personal Memoirs, &c.—continued.

Lejeune.—THE MEMOIRS OF GENERAL LEJEUNE, 1780-1814. Translated by Mrs. ARTHUR BELL (N. D'ANVERS) [In preparation.

Luther.—LIFE OF LUTHER. By JULIUS KÖSTLIN. With Illustrations. Crown 8vo., 7s. 6d.

Macaulay.—THE LIFE AND LETTERS OF LORD MACAULAY. By the Right Hon. Sir G. O. TREVELYAN, Bart., M.P.
Popular Edit. 1 vol. Cr. 8vo., 2s. 6d.
Student's Edition. 1 vol. Cr. 8vo., 6s.
Cabinet Edition. 2vols. Post8vo.,12s.
Library Edition. 2 vols. 8vo., 36s.

Marbot.—THE MEMOIRS OF THE BARON DE MARBOT. Translated from the French by ARTHUR JOHN BUTLER, M.A. Crown 8vo., 7s. 6d.

Romanes.—THE LIFE AND LETTERS OF GEORGE JOHN ROMANES, M.A., LL.D. Written and Edited by his Wife. With Portrait and 2 Illus. 8vo., 15s.

Seebohm.—THE OXFORD REFORMERS —JOHN COLET, ERASMUS AND THOMAS MORE : a History of their Fellow-Work. By FREDERIC SEEBOHM. 8vo., 14s.

Shakespeare.—OUTLINES OF THE LIFE OF SHAKESPEARE. By J. O. HALLIWELL-PHILLIPPS. With numerous Illustrations and Fac-similes. 2 vols. Royal 8vo., £1 1s.

Shakespeare's TRUE LIFE. By JAS. WALTER. With 500 Illustrations by GERALD E. MOIRA. Imp. 8vo., 21s.

Stephen.—ESSAYS IN ECCLESIASTICAL BIOGRAPHY. By Sir JAMES STEPHEN. Crown 8vo., 7s. 6d.

Turgot.—THE LIFE AND WRITINGS OF TURGOT, Comptroller-General of France, 1774-1776. Edited for English Readers by W. WALKER STEPHENS. 8vo.,12s. 6d.

Verney.—MEMOIRS OF THE VERNEY FAMILY.
Vols. I. and II. DURING THE CIVIL WAR. By FRANCES VERNEY. With 38 Portraits. Royal 8vo., 42s.
Vol. III. DURING THE COMMONWEALTH. 1650-1660. By MARGARET M. VERNEY. With 10 Portraits, &c. 8vo., 21s.

Walford.—TWELVE ENGLISH AUTHORESSES. By L. B. WALFORD. Cr.8vo.,4s.6d.

Wellington.—LIFE OF THE DUKE OF WELLINGTON. By the Rev. G. R. GLEIG, M.A. Crown 8vo., 3s. 6d.

Wolf.—THE LIFE OF JOSEPH WOLF, ANIMAL PAINTER. By A. H. Palmer, With 53 Plates and 14 Illustrations in the Text. Royal 8vo, 21s.

Travel and Adventure, the Colonies, &c.

Arnold.—Works by Sir EDWIN ARNOLD, K.C.I.E.
SEAS AND LANDS. With 71 Illustrations. Cr. 8vo., 3s. 6d.
WANDERING WORDS. With 45 Illustrations. 8vo., 18s.
EAST AND WEST. With 41 Illustrations by R. T. PRITCHARD. 8vo., 18s.

**AUSTRALIA AS IT IS, or Facts and Features, Sketches and Incidents of Australia and Australian Life, with Notices of New Zealand. By A CLERGYMAN, thirteen years resident in the interior of New South Wales. Cr. 8vo., 5s.

Baker.—Works by Sir SAMUEL WHITE BAKER.
EIGHT YEARS IN CEYLON. With 6 Illustrations. Crown 8vo., 3s. 6d.
THE RIFLE AND THE HOUND IN CEYLON. 6 Illustrations. Cr. 8vo., 3s. 6d.

Bent.—Works by J. THEODORE BENT.
THE RUINED CITIES OF MASHONALAND : being a Record of Excavation and Exploration in 1891. With Map, 13 Plates, and 104 Illustrations in the Text. Crown 8vo., 3s. 6d.
THE SACRED CITY OF THE ETHIOPIANS: being a Record of Travel and Research in Abyssinia in 1893. With 8 Plates and 65 Illustrations in the Text. 8vo., 18s.

Bicknell.—TRAVEL AND ADVENTURE IN NORTHERN QUEENSLAND. By ARTHUR C. BICKNELL. With 24 Plates and 22 Illustrations in the text. 8vo. 15s.

Brassey.—VOYAGES AND TRAVELS OF LORD BRASSEY, K.C.B., D.C.L., 1862-1894. Arranged and Edited by Captain S. EARDLEY-WILMOT. 2 vols. Cr. 8vo., 10s.

Brassey.—Works by the late LADY BRASSEY.

A VOYAGE IN THE 'SUNBEAM'; OUR HOME ON THE OCEAN FOR ELEVEN MONTHS.

Library Edition. With 8 Maps and Charts, and 118 Illustrations. 8vo., 21s.

Cabinet Edition. With Map and 66 Illustrations. Crown 8vo., 7s. 6d.
Silver Library Edition. With 66 Illustrations. Crown 8vo., 3s. 6d.

Popular Edition. With 60 Illustrations. 4to., 6d. sewed, 1s. cloth.

School Edition. With 37 Illustrations. Fcp., 2s.cloth, or 3s.white parchment.

Travel and Adventure, the Colonies, &c.—*continued.*

Brassey.—Works by the late LADY BRASSEY—*continued.*

SUNSHINE AND STORM IN THE EAST.

Library Edition. With 2 Maps and 141 Illustrations. 8vo., 21*s.*

Cabinet Edition. With 2 Maps and 114 Illustrations. Crown 8vo., 7*s.* 6*d.*

Popular Edition. With 103 Illustrations. 4to., 6*d.* sewed, 1*s.* cloth.

IN THE TRADES, THE TROPICS, AND THE 'ROARING FORTIES'.

Cabinet Edition. With Map and 220 Illustrations. Crown 8vo., 7*s.* 6*d.*

Popular Edition. With 183 Illustrations. 4to., 6*d.* sewed, 1*s.* cloth.

THREE VOYAGES IN THE 'SUNBEAM'. Popular Edition. 346 Illustrations. 4to., 2*s.* 6*d.*

Froude.—Works by JAMES A. FROUDE.

OCEANA : or England and her Colonies. With 9 Illustrations. Crown 8vo., 2*s.* boards, 2*s.* 6*d.* cloth.

THE ENGLISH IN THE WEST INDIES : or the Bow of Ulysses. With 9 Illustrations. Cr. 8vo., 2*s.* bds., 2*s.* 6*d.* cl.

Howitt.—VISITS TO REMARKABLE PLACES, Old Halls, Battle-Fields, Scenes illustrative of Striking Passages in English History and Poetry. By WILLIAM HOWITT. With 80 Illustrations. Crown 8vo., 3*s.* 6*d.*

Knight.—Works by E. F. KNIGHT.

THE CRUISE OF THE 'ALERTE': the Narrative of a Search for Treasure on the Desert Island of Trinidad. 2 Maps and 23 Illustrations. Cr. 8vo., 3*s.* 6*d.*

WHERE THREE EMPIRES MEET: a Narrative of Recent Travel in Kashmir, Western Tibet, Baltistan, Ladak, Gilgit, and the adjoining Countries. With a Map and 54 Illustrations. Cr. 8vo., 3*s.* 6*d.*

THE 'FALCON' ON THE BALTIC: being a Voyage from London to Copenhagen in a Three-Tonner. With 10 Full-page Illustrations. Crown 8vo., 3*s.* 6*d.*

Lees and Clutterbuck.—B. C. 1887: A RAMBLE IN BRITISH COLUMBIA. By J. A. LEES and W. J. CLUTTERBUCK. With Map and 75 Illustrations. Cr. 8vo., 3*s.* 6*d.*

Murdoch.—FROM EDINBURGH TO THE ANTARCTIC: An Artist's Notes and Sketches during the Dundee Antarctic Expedition of 1892-93. By W. G. BURN MURDOCH. With 2 Maps and numerous Illustrations. 8vo., 18*s*

Nansen.—Works by Dr. FRIDTJOF NANSEN.

THE FIRST CROSSING OF GREENLAND. With numerous Illustrations and a Map. Crown 8vo., 3*s.* 6*d.*

ESKIMO LIFE. Translated by WILLIAM ARCHER. With 31 Illustrations. 8vo., 16*s.*

Peary.—MY ARCTIC JOURNAL: a Year among Ice-Fields and Eskimos. By JOSEPHINE DIEBITSCH-PEARY. With 19 Plates, 3 Sketch Maps, and 44 Illustrations in the Text. 8vo., 12*s.*

Quillinan. — JOURNAL OF A FEW MONTHS' RESIDENCE IN PORTUGAL, and Glimpses of the South of Spain. By Mrs. QUILLINAN (Dora Wordsworth). New Edition. Edited, with Memoir, by EDMUND LEE, Author of 'Dorothy Wordsworth.' etc. Crown 8vo., 6*s.*

Smith.—CLIMBING IN THE BRITISH ISLES. By W. P. HASKETT SMITH. With Illustrations by ELLIS CARR.

Part I. ENGLAND. 16mo., 3*s.* 6*d.*

Part II. WALES AND IRELAND. 16mo., 3*s.* 6*d.*

Part III. SCOTLAND. [*In preparation.*

Stephen. — THE PLAYGROUND OF EUROPE. By LESLIE STEPHEN, formerly President of the Alpine Club. New Edition, with Additions and 4 Illustrations. Crown 8vo., 6*s.* net.

THREE IN NORWAY. By Two of Them. With a Map and 59 Illustrations. Cr. 8vo., 2*s.* boards, 2*s.* 6*d.* cloth.

Tyndall.—THE GLACIERS OF THE ALPS: being a Narrative of Excursions and Ascents. An Account of the Origin and Phenomena of Glaciers, and an Exposition of the Physical Principles to which they are related. By JOHN TYNDALL, F.R.S. With numerous Illustrations. Crown 8vo., 6*s.* 6*d.* net.

Whishaw. — Works by FRED. J. WHISHAW.

THE ROMANCE OF THE WOODS: Reprinted Articles and Sketches. Crown 8vo., 6*s.*

OUT OF DOORS IN TSARLAND: a Record of the Seeings and Doings of a Wanderer in Russia. Cr. 8vo., 7*s.* 6*d.*

Sport and Pastime.

THE BADMINTON LIBRARY.

Crown 8vo., 10s. 6d., each volume.

Edited by the DUKE OF BEAUFORT, K.G., assisted by ALFRED E. T. WATSON.

ARCHERY. By C. J. LONGMAN and Col. H. WALROND, &c. 195 Illusts.

ATHLETICS AND FOOTBALL. By MONTAGUE SHEARMAN. 51 Illusts.

BIG GAME SHOOTING. By C. PHIL-LIPPS-WOLLEY, F. C. SELOUS, &c. Vol. I. Africa and America. With 77 Illus.
Vol. II. Europe, Asia, and the Arctic Regions. With 73 Illustrations.

BILLIARDS. By Major W. BROADFOOT, R.E., &c. With 30 Illustrations and numerous Diagrams and Figures.

BOATING. By W. B. WOODGATE. With 49 Illustrations.

COURSING AND FALCONRY. By HARDING COX and the Hon. GERALD LASCELLES. With 76 Illustrations.

CRICKET. By A. G. STEEL, the Hon. R. H. LYTTELTON, ANDREW LANG, W. G. GRACE, &c. With 64 Illustrations.

CYCLING. By the Earl of Albemarle and G. LACY HILLIER. With 59 Illus.

DANCING. By Mrs. LILLY GROVE, F.R.G.S., &c. With 131 Illustrations.

DRIVING. By the DUKE OF BEAUFORT. With 65 Illustrations.

FENCING, BOXING, AND WREST-LING. By WALTER H. POLLOCK, F. C. GROVE, WALTER ARMSTRONG. With 42 Illustrations.

FISHING. By H. CHOLMONDELEY-PEN-NELL, the MARQUIS OF EXETER, G. CHRISTOPHER DAVIES, &c. Vol. I. Salmon, Trout, and Grayling. With 158 Illustrations.
Vol. II. Pike and other Coarse Fish. With 133 Illustrations.

GOLF. By HORACE G. HUTCHINSON, the Rt. Hon. A. J. BALFOUR, M.P., Sir W. G. SIMPSON, Bart., ANDREW LANG, &c. With 89 Illustrations.

HUNTING. By the DUKE OF BEAUFORT, K.G., MOWBRAY MORRIS, the EARL OF SUFFOLK AND BERKSHIRE, ALFRED E. T. WATSON, &c. 53 Illustrations.

MOUNTAINEERING. By C. T. DENT, Sir F. POLLOCK, Bart., W. M. CONWAY, DOUGLAS FRESHFIELD, C. E. MA-THEWS, &c. With 108 Illustrations.

RACING AND STEEPLE-CHASING. By the EARL OF SUFFOLK AND BERK-SHIRE, ARTHUR COVENTRY, &c. With 58 Illustrations.

RIDING AND POLO. By Captain ROBERT WEIR, J. MORAY BROWN, the DUKE OF BEAUFORT, K.G., the EARL of SUFFOLK AND BERKSHIRE, &c. With 59 Illustrations.

SEA FISHING. By JOHN BICKERDYKE. With Contributions by Sir H. GORE-BOOTH, Bart., ALFRED C. HARMS-WORTH, and W. SENIOR. With 197 Illustrations.

SHOOTING. By Lord WALSINGHAM and Sir RALPH PAYNE-GALLWEY, Bart. LORD LOVAT, LORD C. L. KERR, and A. J. STUART-WORTLEY, &c. Vol. I. Field and Covert. With 105 Illustrations.
Vol. II. Moor and Marsh. With 65 Illustrations.

SKATING, CURLING, TOBOGA-NING, AND OTHER ICE SPORTS. By J. M. HEATHCOTE, C. G. TEBBUTT, T. MAXWELL WITHAM, the Rev. JOHN KERR, &c. With 284 Illustrations.

SWIMMING. By ARCHIBALD SINCLAIR and WILLIAM HENRY. With 119 Illus.

TENNIS, LAWN TENNIS, RAC-QUETS, AND FIVES. By J. M. and C. G. HEATHCOTE, E. O. PLEYDELL-BOUVERIE, the Hon. A. LYTTELTON, Miss L. DOD, &c. With 79 Illustrations.

YACHTING.
Vol. I. Cruising, Construction, Racing, Rules, Fitting-Out, &c. By Sir EDWARD SULLIVAN, Bart., LORD BRASSEY, K.C.B., C. E. SETH-SMITH, C.B., &c. With 114 Illustrations.
Vol. II. Yacht Clubs, Yachting in America and the Colonies, Yacht Rac-ing, &c. By R. T. PRITCHETT, the EARL OF ONSLOW, G.C.M.G., &c. With 195 Illustrations.

Sport and Pastime—*continued.*
FUR AND FEATHER SERIES.
Edited by A. E. T. WATSON.
Crown 8vo., 5s. each Volume.

THE PARTRIDGE. Natural History, by the Rev. H. A. MACPHERSON; Shooting, by A. J. STUART-WORTLEY; Cookery, by GEORGE SAINTSBURY. With 11 Illustrations and various Diagrams.

THE GROUSE. Natural History by the Rev. H. A. MACPHERSON; Shooting, by A. J. STUART-WORTLEY; Cookery, by GEORGE SAINTSBURY. With 13 Illustrations and various Diagrams.

THE PHEASANT. Natural History by the Rev. H A. MACPHERSON; Shooting, by A. J STUART-WORTLEY. Cookery, by ALEXANDER INNES SHAND With 10 Illustrations and various Diagrams.

THE HARE. By the Hon. GERALD LASCELLES, &c. [*In preparation.*

WILDFOWL By the HON. JOHN SCOTT-MONTAGU. M P., &c. [*In preparation.*

THE RED DEER. By CAMERON OF LOCHIEL, LORD EBRINGTON, &c. [*In preparation.*

BADMINTON MAGAZINE OF SPORTS AND PASTIMES, THE. Edited by ALFRED E. E. WATSON ('Rapier'). With numerous Illustrations, 1s. Monthly. Vol. I., August to December, 1895. 6s.

Bickerdyke.—DAYS OF MY LIFE ON WATERS FRESH AND SALT; and other Papers. By JOHN BICKERDYKE. With Photo-Etched Frontispiece and 8 Full-page Illustrations. Crown 8vo., 6s.

Campbell-Walker.—THE CORRECT CARD: or, How to Play at Whist; a Whist Catechism. By Major A. CAMPBELL-WALKER. Fcp. 8vo., 2s. 6d.

DEAD SHOT (THE): or, Sportsman's Complete Guide. Being a Treatise on the Use of the Gun, with Rudimentary and Finishing Lessons on the Art of Shooting Game of all kinds. By MARKSMAN. With 13 Illustrations. Crown 8vo., 10s. 6d.

Ellis.—CHESS SPARKS; or, Short and Bright Games of Chess. Collected and Arranged by J. H. ELLIS, M.A. 8vo., 4s. 6d.

Falkener.—GAMES, ANCIENT AND ORIENTAL, AND HOW TO PLAY THEM. By EDWARD FALKENER. With numerous Photographs & Diagrams. 8vo., 21s.

Ford.—THE THEORY AND PRACTICE OF ARCHERY. By HORACE FORD. New Edition, thoroughly Revised and Re-written by W. BUTT, M.A. With a Preface by C. J. LONGMAN, M.A. 8vo., 14s.

Francis.—A BOOK ON ANGLING: or, Treatise on the Art of Fishing in every Branch; including full Illustrated List of Salmon Flies. By FRANCIS FRANCIS. With Portrait and Plates. Cr. 8vo., 15s.

Gibson.—TOBOGGANING ON CROOKED RUNS. By the Hon. HARRY GIBSON. With Contributions by F. DE B. STRICKLAND and 'LADY-TOBOGGANER'. With 40 Illustrations. Crown 8vo., 6s.

Hawker.—THE DIARY OF COLONEL PETER HAWKER, author of "Instructions to Young Sportsmen". With an Introduction by Sir RALPH PAYNE-GALLWEY, Bart. 2 vols. 8vo., 32s.

Lang.—ANGLING SKETCHES. By A. LANG. With 20 Illus Cr. 8vo., 3s. 6d.

Longman.—CHESS OPENINGS. By FRED. W. LONGMAN. Fcp. 8vo., 2s. 6d.

Maskelyne.—SHARPS AND FLATS a Complete Revelation of the Secrets of Cheating at Games of Chance and Skill. By JOHN NEVIL MASKELYNE. With 62 Illustrations. Crown 8vo., 6s.

Park.—THE GAME OF GOLF. By WILLIAM PARK, Junr. Champion Golfer, 1887-89. With 17 Plates and 26 Illustrations in the Text. Crown 8vo., 7s. 6d.

Payne-Gallwey. — Works by Sir RALPH PAYNE-GALLWEY, Bart.
LETTERS TO YOUNG SHOOTERS (First Series). On the Choice and Use of a Gun. With 41 Illustrations. Cr. 8vo., 7s. 6d.
LETTERS TO YOUNG SHOOTERS. (Second Series). On the Production, Preservation, and Killing of Game. With Directions in Shooting Wood-Pigeons and Breaking-in Retrievers. With 104 Illustrations. Crown 8vo., 12s. 6d.

Pole.—Works by W. POLE, F.R.S.
THE THEORY OF THE MODERN SCIENTIFIC GAME OF WHIST. Fcp. 8vo., 2s. 6d.
THE EVOLUTION OF WHIST. Cr. 8vo., 6s.

Proctor.—Works by R. A. PROCTOR.
HOW TO PLAY WHIST: WITH THE LAWS AND ETIQUETTE OF WHIST. Crown 8vo., 3s. 6d.
HOME WHIST: an Easy Guide to Correct Play. 16mo., 1s.

Ronalds.—THE FLY-FISHER'S ENTOMOLOGY. By ALFRED RONALDS. With 20 Coloured Plates. 8vo., 14s.

Wilcocks. THE SEA FISHERMAN: Comprising the Chief Methods of Hook and Line Fishing in the British and other Seas, and Remarks on Nets, Boats, and Boating. By J. C. WILCOCKS. Illustrated. Crown 8vo., 6s.

Veterinary Medicine, &c.

Steel.—Works by JOHN HENRY STEEL,
A TREATISE ON THE DISEASES OF THE
DOG. 88 Illustrations. 8vo., 10s. 6d.

A TREATISE ON THE DISEASES OF
THE OX. With 119 Illustrations.
8vo., 15s.

A TREATISE ON THE DISEASES OF THE
SHEEP. With 100 Illustrations. 8vo.,
12s.

OUTLINES OF EQUINE ANATOMY: a
Manual for the use of Veterinary
Students in the Dissecting Room.
Crown 8vo, 7s. 6d.

Fitzwygram.--HORSES AND STABLES.
By Major-General Sir F. FITZWYGRAM,
Bart. With 56 pages of Illustrations.
8vo., 2s. 6d. net.

"Stonehenge."—THE DOG IN HEALTH
AND DISEASE. By "STONEHENGE ".
With 78 Illustrations 8vo., 7s. 6d.

Youatt.—Works by WILLIAM YOUATT.
THE HORSE. With 52 Illustrations.
8vo., 7s. 6d.
THE DOG. With 53 Illustrations.
8vo., 6s.

Mental, Moral, and Political Philosophy.
LOGIC, RHETORIC, PSYCHOLOGY, ETC.

Abbott.—THE ELEMENTS OF LOGIC. By
T. K. ABBOTT, B.D. 12mo., 3s.

Aristotle.—Works by.
THE POLITICS: G. Bekker's Greek Text
of Books I., III., IV. (VII.), with an
English Translation by W. E. BOL-
LAND, M.A.; and short Introductory
Essays by A. LANG, M.A. Crown
8vo., 7s. 6d.

THE POLITICS: Introductory Essays.
By ANDREW LANG (from Bolland and
Lang's ' Politics '). Cr. 8vo., 2s. 6d.

THE ETHICS: Greek Text, Illustrated
with Essay and Notes. By Sir ALEX-
ANDER GRANT, Bart. 2 vols. 8vo., 32s.

THE NICOMACHEAN ETHICS: Newly
Translated into English. By ROBERT
WILLIAMS. Crown 8vo., 7s. 6d.

AN INTRODUCTION TO ARISTOTLE'S
ETHICS. Books I.-IV. (Book X. c.
vi.-ix. in an Appendix.) With a con-
tinuous Analysis and Notes. By the
Rev. E. MOORE, D.D. Cr. 8vo., 10s. 6d.

Bacon.—Works by FRANCIS BACON.
COMPLETE WORKS. Edited by R. L.
ELLIS, J. SPEDDING, and D. D.
HEATH. 7 vols. 8vo., £3 13s. 6d.

LETTERS AND LIFE, including all his
occasional Works. Edited by JAMES
SPEDDING. 7 vols. 8vo., £4 4s.

THE ESSAYS: with Annotations. By
RICHARD WHATELY, D.D. 8vo.
10s. 6d.

THE ESSAYS: Edited, with Notes. By
F. STORR and C. H. GIBSON. Cr.
8vo., 3s. 6d.

THE ESSAYS. With Introduction, Notes,
and Index. By E. A. ABBOTT. D.D.
2 vols. Fcp. 8vo., 6s. The Text and
Index only, without Introduction and
Notes, in One Volume. Fcp. 8vo.,
2s. 6d.

Bain.—Works by ALEXANDER BAIN,
LL.D.
MENTAL SCIENCE. Crown 8vo., 6s. 6d.
MORAL SCIENCE. Crown 8vo., 4s. 6d.
*The two works as above can be had in one
volume, price 10s. 6d.*
SENSES AND THE INTELLECT. 8vo., 15s.
EMOTIONS AND THE WILL. 8vo., 15s.
LOGIC, DEDUCTIVE AND INDUCTIVE.
Part I., 4s. Part II., 6s. 6d.
PRACTICAL ESSAYS. Crown 8vo., 3s.

Bray.—Works by CHARLES BRAY.
THE PHILOSOPHY OF NECESSITY : or
Law in Mind as in Matter. Cr. 8vo., 5s.
THE EDUCATION OF THE FEELINGS : a
Moral System for Schools. Crown
8vo., 2s. 6d.

Bray.—ELEMENTS OF MORALITY, in
Easy Lessons for Home and School
Teaching. By Mrs. CHARLES BRAY.
Cr. 8vo., 1s. 6d.

Davidson.—THE LOGIC OF DEFINI-
TION, Explained and Applied. By
WILLIAM L. DAVIDSON, M.A. Crown
8vo., 6s.

Green.—THE WORKS OF THOMAS HILL
GREEN. Edited by R. L. NETTLESHIP.
Vols. I. and II. Philosophical Works.
8vo., 16s. each.
Vol. III. Miscellanies. With Index to
the three Volumes, and Memoir. 8vo.,
21s.

LECTURES ON THE PRINCIPLES OF
POLITICAL OBLIGATION. With
Preface by BERNARD BOSANQUET.
8vo., 5s.

Mental, Moral and Political Philosophy—*continued*.

Hodgson.—Works by SHADWORTH H. HODGSON.
TIME AND SPACE: a Metaphysical Essay. 8vo., 16s.
THE THEORY OF PRACTICE : an Ethical Inquiry. 2 vols. 8vo., 24s.
THE PHILOSOPHY OF REFLECTION. 2 vols. 8vo., 21s.

Hume.—THE PHILOSOPHICAL WORKS OF DAVID HUME. Edited by T. H. GREEN and T. H. GROSE. 4 vols. 8vo., 56s. Or separately, Essays. 2 vols. 28s. Treatise of Human Nature. 2 vols. 28s.

Justinian.—THE INSTITUTES OF JUSTINIAN: Latin Text, chiefly that of Huschke, with English Introduction, Translation, Notes, and Summary. By THOMAS C. SANDARS, M.A. 8vo. 18s.

Kant.—Works by IMMANUEL KANT.
CRITIQUE OF PRACTICAL REASON, AND OTHER WORKS ON THE THEORY OF ETHICS. Translated by T. K. ABBOTT, B.D. With Memoir. 8vo., 12s. 6d.
FUNDAMENTAL PRINCIPLES OF THE METAPHYSIC OF ETHICS. Translated by T. K. ABBOTT, B.D. (Extracted from ' Kant's Critique of Practical Reason and other Works on the Theory of Ethics.' Cr. 8vo. 3s.
INTRODUCTION TO LOGIC, AND HIS ESSAY ON THE MISTAKEN SUBTILTY OF THE FOUR FIGURES. Translated by T. K. ABBOTT, and with Notes by S. T. COLERIDGE. 8vo., 6s.

Killick.—HANDBOOK TO MILL'S SYSTEM OF LOGIC. By Rev. A. H. KILLICK, M.A. Crown 8vo., 3s. 6d.

Ladd.—Works by GEORGE TURMBULL LADD.
ELEMENTS OF PHYSIOLOGICAL PSYCHOLOGY. 8vo., 21s.
OUTLINES OF PHYSIOLOGICAL PSYCHOLOGY. A Text-Book of Mental Science for Academies and Colleges. 8vo., 12s.
PSYCHOLOGY, DESCRIPTIVE AND EXPLANATORY : a Treatise of the Phenomena, Laws, and Development of Human Mental Life. 8vo., 21s.
PRIMER OF PSYCHOLOGY. Crown 8vo., 5s. 6d.
PHILOSOPHY OF MIND: an Essay on the Metaphysics of Physiology. 8vo., 16s.

Lewes.—THE HISTORY OF PHILOSOPHY, from Thales to Comte. By GEORGE HENRY LEWES. 2 vols. 8vo., 32s.

Max Müller.—Works by F. MAX MÜLLER.
THE SCIENCE OF THOUGHT. 8vo., 21s.
THREE INTRODUCTORY LECTURES ON THE SCIENCE OF THOUGHT. 8vo., 2s. 6d.

Mosso.—FEAR. By ANGELO MOSSO. Translated from the Italian by E. LOUGH and F. KIESOW. With 8 Illustrations. Crown 8vo., 7s. 6d.

Mill.—ANALYSIS OF THE PHENOMENA OF THE HUMAN MIND. By JAMES MILL. 2 vols. 8vo., 28s.

Mill.—Works by JOHN STUART MILL.
A SYSTEM OF LOGIC. Cr. 8vo., 3s. 6d.
ON LIBERTY. Cr. 8vo., 1s. 4d.
ON REPRESENTATIVE GOVERNMENT. Crown 8vo., 2s.
UTILITARIANISM. 8vo., 2s. 6d.
EXAMINATION OF SIR WILLIAM HAMILTON'S PHILOSOPHY. 8vo., 16s.
NATURE, THE UTILITY OF RELIGION, AND THEISM. Three Essays. 8vo., 5s.

Romanes.—MIND AND MOTION AND MONISM. By: he late GEORGE JOHN ROMANES, M.A., LL.D., F.R.S. Cr. 8vo., 4s. 6d.

Stock.—DEDUCTIVE LOGIC. By ST. GEORGE STOCK. Fcp. 8vo., 3s. 6d.

Sully.—Works by JAMES SULLY.
THE HUMAN MIND : a Text-book of Psychology. 2 vols. 8vo., 21s.
OUTLINES OF PSYCHOLOGY. 8vo., 9s.
THE TEACHER'S HANDBOOK OF PSYCHOLOGY. Crown 8vo., 5s.
STUDIES OF CHILDHOOD. 8vo. 10s. 6d.

Swinburne.—PICTURE LOGIC: an Attempt to Popularise the Science of Reasoning. By ALFRED JAMES SWINBURNE, M.A. With 23 Woodcuts. Post 8vo., 5s.

Thomson.—OUTLINES OF THE NECESSARY LAWS OF THOUGHT: a Treatise on Pure and Applied Logic. By WILLIAM THOMSON, D.D., formerly Lord Archbishop of York. Post 8vo., 6s.

Mental, Moral and Political Philosophy—*continued.*

Whately.—Works by R. WHATELY, D.D.

BACON'S ESSAYS. With Annotation. By R. WHATELY. 8vo., 10s. 6d.

ELEMENTS OF LOGIC. Cr. 8vo., 4s. 6d.

ELEMENTS OF RHETORIC. Cr. 8vo., 4s. 6d.

LESSONS ON REASONING. Fcp. 8vo., 1s. 6d.

Zeller.—Works by Dr. EDWARD ZELLER, Professor in the University of Berlin.

THE STOICS, EPICUREANS, AND SCEPTICS. Translated by the Rev. O. J. REICHEL, M.A. Crown 8vo., 15s.

Zeller.—Works by Dr. EDWARD ZELLER. —*continued.*

OUTLINES OF THE HISTORY OF GREEK PHILOSOPHY. Translated by SARAH F. ALLEYNE and EVELYN ABBOTT. Crown 8vo., 10s. 6d.

PLATO AND THE OLDER ACADEMY. Translated by SARAH F ALLEYNE and ALFRED GOODWIN, B.A. Crown 8vo., 18s.

SOCRATES AND THE SOCRATIC SCHOOLS. Translated by the Rev. O. J. REICHEL, M.A. Crown 8vo., 10s. 6d.

MANUALS OF CATHOLIC PHILOSOPHY.

(Stonyhurst Series.)

A MANUAL OF POLITICAL ECONOMY. By C. S. DEVAS, M.A. Cr. 8vo., 6s. 6d.

FIRST PRINCIPLES OF KNOWLEDGE. By JOHN RICKABY, S.J. Crown 8vo., 5s.

GENERAL METAPHYSICS. By JOHN RICKABY, S.J. Crown 8vo., 5s.

LOGIC. By RICHARD F. CLARKE, S.J. Crown 8vo., 5s.

MORAL PHILOSOPHY (ETHICS AND NATURAL LAW). By JOSEPH RICKABY, S.J. Crown 8vo., 5s.

NATURAL THEOLOGY. By BERNARD BOEDDER, S.J. Crown 8vo., 6s. 6d.

PSYCHOLOGY. By MICHAEL MAHER, S.J. Crown 8vo., 6s. 6d.

History and Science of Language, &c.

Davidson.—LEADING AND IMPORTANT ENGLISH WORDS: Explained and Exemplified. By WILLIAM L. DAVIDSON, M.A. Fcp. 8vo., 3s. 6d.

Farrar.—LANGUAGE AND LANGUAGES. By F. W. FARRAR, D.D., F.R.S., Cr. 8vo., 6s.

Graham.—ENGLISH SYNONYMS, Classified and Explained: with Practical Exercises. By G. F. GRAHAM. Fcap. 8vo., 6s.

Max Müller.—Works by F. MAX MÜLLER.

THE SCIENCE OF LANGUAGE, Founded on Lectures delivered at the Royal Institution in 1861 and 1863. 2 vols. Crown 8vo., 21s.

BIOGRAPHIES OF WORDS, AND THE HOME OF THE ARYAS. Crown 8vo., 7s. 6d.

Max Müller.—Works by F. MAX MÜLLER—*continued.*

THREE LECTURES ON THE SCIENCE OF LANGUAGE, AND ITS PLACE IN GENERAL EDUCATION, delivered at Oxford, 1889. Crown 8vo., 3s.

Roget.—THESAURUS OF ENGLISH WORDS AND PHRASES. Classified and Arranged so as to Facilitate the Expression of Ideas and assist in Literary Composition. By PETER MARK ROGET, M.D., F.R.S. Recomposed throughout, enlarged and improved, partly from the Author's Notes, and with a full Index, by the Author's Son, JOHN LEWIS ROGET. Crown 8vo., 10s. 6d.

Whately.—ENGLISH SYNONYMS. By E. JANE WHATELY. Fcap. 8vo., 3s.

Political Economy and Economics.

Ashley.—ENGLISH ECONOMIC HISTORY AND THEORY. By W. J. ASHLEY, M.A. Crown 8vo., Part I., 5s. Part II., 10s. 6d.

Bagehot.—ECONOMIC STUDIES. By WALTER BAGEHOT. Cr. 8vo., 3s. 6d.

Barnett.—PRACTICABLE SOCIALISM : Essays on Social Reform. By the Rev. S. A. and Mrs. BARNETT. Cr. 8vo., 6s.

Brassey.—PAPERS AND ADDRESSES ON WORK AND WAGES. By Lord BRASSEY. Crown 8vo., 5s.

Devas.—A MANUAL OF POLITICAL ECONOMY. By C. S. DEVAS, M.A. Crown 8vo., 6s. 6d. (*Manuals of Catholic Philosophy.*)

Dowell.—A HISTORY OF TAXATION AND TAXES IN ENGLAND, from the Earliest Times to the Year 1885. By STEPHEN DOWELL (4 vols. 8vo.) Vols. I. and II. The History of Taxation, 21s. Vols. III. and IV. The History of Taxes, 21s.

HANDBOOKS OF ECONOMICS AND POLITICAL SCIENCE. Issued under the auspices of the London School of Economics and Political Science.
THE HISTORY OF LOCAL RATES IN ENGLAND. By EDWIN CANNAN, M.A. Crown 8vo., 2s. 6d.
* *Other Volumes of this Series are in Preparation.*

Macleod.—Works by HENRY DUNNING MACLEOD, M.A.
BIMETALISM. 8vo., 5s. net.
ELEMENTS OF BANKING. Cr.8vo.,3s.6d.
THE THEORY AND PRACTICE OF BANKING. Vol. I. 8vo., 12s. Vol. II. 14s.
THE THEORY OF CREDIT. 8vo. Vol. I. 10s. net. Vol. II., Part I., 10s. net. Vol. II. Part II., 10s. 6d.
A DIGEST OF THE LAW OF BILLS OF EXCHANGE, BANK NOTES, &c.

Mill.—POLITICAL ECONOMY. By JOHN STUART MILL.
Popular Edition. Crown 8vo., 3s 6d.
Library Edition. 2 vols. 8vo., 30s.

Symes.—POLITICAL ECONOMY: a Short Text-book of Political Economy. With Problems for Solution, and Hints for Supplementary Reading. By Prof. J. E. SYMES, M.A., of University College, Nottingham. Crown 8vo., 2s. 6d.

Toynbee.—LECTURES ON THE INDUSTRIAL REVOLUTION OF THE 18th CENTURY IN ENGLAND. By ARNOLD TOYNBEE. With a Memoir of the Author by BENJAMIN JOWETT, D.D. 8vo., 10s. 6d.

Webb.—THE HISTORY OF TRADE UNIONISM. By SIDNEY and BEATRICE WEBB. With Map and full Bibliography of the Subject. 8vo., 18s.

Evolution, Anthropology, &c.

Babington. — FALLACIES OF RACE THEORIES AS APPLIED TO NATIONAL CHARACTERISTICS. Essays by WILLIAM DALTON BABINGTON, M.A. Crown 8vo., 6s.

Clodd.—Works by EDWARD CLODD.
THE STORY OF CREATION : a Plain Account of Evolution. With 77 Illustrations. Crown 8vo., 3s. 6d.
A PRIMER OF EVOLUTION : being a Popular Abridged Edition of 'The Story of Creation'. With Illustrations. Fcp. 8vo., 1s. 6d.

Lang.—CUSTOM AND MYTH : Studies of Early Usage and Belief. By ANDREW LANG, M.A. With 15 Illustrations. Crown 8vo., 3s. 6d.

Lubbock.—THE ORIGIN OF CIVILISATION and the Primitive Condition of Man. By Sir J. LUBBOCK, Bart., M.P. With 5 Plates and 20 Illustrations in the Text. 8vo. 18s.

Romanes.—Works by GEORGE JOHN ROMANES, M.A., LL.D., F.R.S.
DARWIN, AND AFTER DARWIN : an Exposition of the Darwinian Theory, and a Discussion on Post-Darwinian Questions.
Part I. THE DARWINIAN THEORY. With Portrait of Darwin and 125 Illustrations. Crown 8vo., 10s. 6d.
Part II. POST-DARWINIAN QUESTIONS : Heredity and Utility. With Portrait of the Author and 5 Illustrations. Cr. 8vo., 10s. 6d.
AN EXAMINATION OF WEISMANNISM. Crown 8vo., 6s.
MIND AND MOTION AND MONISM. Crown 8vo., 4s. 6d.

Classical Literature and Translations, &c.

Abbott.—HÉLLENICA. A Collection of Essays on Greek Poetry, Philosophy, History, and Religion. Edited by EVELYN ABBOTT, M.A., LL.D. 8vo., 16s.

Æschylus.—EUMENIDES OF ÆSCHYLUS. With Metrical English Translation. By J. F. DAVIES. 8vo., 7s.

Aristophanes.—The ACHARNIANS OF ARISTOPHANES, translated into English Verse. By R. Y. TYRRELL. Cr. 8vo., 1s.

Becker.—Works by Professor BECKER.

GALLUS: or, Roman Scenes in the Time of Augustus. Illustrated. Cr. 8vo., 3s. 6d.

CHARICLES: or, Illustrations of the Private Life of the Ancient Greeks. Illustrated. Cr 8vo., 3s. 6d.

Cicero.—CICERO'S CORRESPONDENCE. By R. Y. TYRRELL. Vols. I., II., III. 8vo., each 12s. Vol. IV., 15s.

Farnell.—GREEK LYRIC POETRY: a Complete Collection of the Surviving Passages from the Greek Song-Writing. By GEORGE S. FARNELL, M.A. With 5 Plates. 8vo., 16s.

Lang.—HOMER AND THE EPIC. By ANDREW LANG. Crown 8vo., 9s. net.

Mackail.—SELECT EPIGRAMS FROM THE GREEK ANTHOLOGY. By J. W. MACKAIL 8vo., 16s.

Rich.—A DICTIONARY OF ROMAN AND GREEK ANTIQUITIES. By A. RICH, B.A. With 2000 Woodcuts. Crown 8vo., 7s. 6d.

Sophocles.—Translated into English Verse. By ROBERT WHITELAW, M.A., Assistant Master in Rugby School: late Fellow of Trinity College, Cambridge. Crown 8vo., 8s. 6d.

Tyrrell—TRANSLATIONS INTO GREEK AND LATIN VERSE. Edited by R. Y. TYRRELL. 8vo., 6s.

Virgil.—THE ÆNEID OF VIRGIL. Translated into English Verse by JOHN CONINGTON. Crown 8vo., 6s.

THE POEMS OF VIRGIL. Translated into English Prose by JOHN CONINGTON. Crown 8vo., 6s.

THE ÆNEID OF VIRGIL, freely translated into English Blank Verse. By W. J. THORNHILL. Crown 8vo., 7s. 6d.

THE ÆNEID OF VIRGIL. Books I. to VI. Translated into English Verse by JAMES RHOADES. Crown 8vo., 5s.

Wilkins.—THE GROWTH OF THE HOMERIC POEMS. By G. WILKINS. 8vo. 6s.

Poetry and the Drama.

Acworth.—BALLADS OF THE MARATHAS. Rendered into English Verse from the Marathi Originals. By HARRY ARBUTHNOT ACWORTH. 8vo., 5s.

Allingham.—Works by WILLIAM ALLINGHAM.

BLACKBERRIES. Imperial 16mo., 6s.

IRISH SONGS AND POEMS. With Frontispiece of the Waterfall of Asaroe. Fcp. 8vo., 6s.

LAURENCE BLOOMFIELD. With Portrait of the Author. Fcp. 8vo., 3s. 6d.

Allingham. — Works by WILLIAM ALLINGHAM—*continued.*

FLOWER PIECES; DAY AND NIGHT SONGS; BALLADS. With 2 Designs by D. G. ROSSETTI. Fcp. 8vo., 6s.; large paper edition, 12s.

LIFE AND PHANTASY: with Frontispiece by Sir J. E. MILLAIS, Bart., and Design by ARTHUR HUGHES. Fcp. 8vo., 6s.; large paper edition, 12s.

THOUGHT AND WORD, AND ASHBY MANOR: a Play. Fcp. 8vo., 6s.; large paper edition, 12s.

Sets of the above 6 vols. may be had in uniform half-parchment binding, price 30s.

Poetry and the Drama—*continued.*

Armstrong.—Works by G. F. SAVAGE-ARMSTRONG.

POEMS : Lyrical and Dramatic. Fcp. 8vo., 6s.

KING SAUL. (The Tragedy of Israel, Part I.) Fcp. 8vo. 5s.

KING DAVID. (The Tragedy of Israel, Part II.) Fcp. 8vo., 6s.

KING SOLOMON. (The Tragedy of Israel, Part III.) Fcp. 8vo., 6s.

UGONE : a Tragedy. Fcp. 8vo., 6s.

A GARLAND FROM GREECE : Poems. Fcp. 8vo., 7s. 6d.

STORIES OF WICKLOW : Poems. Fcp. 8vo., 7s. 6d.

MEPHISTOPHELES IN BROADCLOTH : a Satire. Fcp. 8vo., 4s.

ONE IN THE INFINITE : a Poem. Cr. 8vo., 7s. 6d.

Armstrong.—THE POETICAL WORKS OF EDMUND J. ARMSTRONG. Fcp. 8vo., 5s.

Arnold.—Works by Sir EDWIN ARNOLD, K.C.I.E.

THE LIGHT OF THE WORLD : or, the Great Consummation. Cr. 8vo.,7s. 6d. net.

THE TENTH MUSE, AND OTHER POEMS. Crown 8vo., 5s. net.

POTIPHAR'S WIFE, and other Poems. Crown 8vo., 5s. net.

ADZUMA : or, the Japanese Wife. A Play. Crown 8vo., 6s. 6d. net.

Beesly.—BALLADS, AND OTHER VERSE. By A. H. BEESLY. Fcp. 8vo., 5s.

Bell.—CHAMBER COMEDIES : a Collection of Plays and Monologues for the Drawing Room. By Mrs. HUGH BELL. Crown 8vo., 6s.

Carmichael.—POEMS. By JENNINGS CARMICHAEL (Mrs. FRANCIS MULLIS). Crown 8vo, 6s. net.

Cochrane.—Works by ALFRED COCHRANE.

THE KESTREL'S NEST,and other Verses. Fcp. 8vo., 3s. 6d.

LEVIORE PLECTRO : Occasional Verses. Fcp. 8vo., 3s. 6d.

Florian.—THE FABLES OF FLORIAN. Done into English Verse by Sir PHILIP PERRING, Bart. Crown 8vo., 3s. 6d.

Goethe.

FAUST, Part I., the German Text, with Introduction and Notes. By ALBERT M. SELSS, Ph.D., M.A. Cr. 8vo., 5s.

FAUST. Translated, with Notes. By T. E. WEBB. 8vo., 12s. 6d.

Gurney.—DAY DREAMS : Poems. By Rev. ALFRED GURNEY. M.A. Crown 8vo, 3s. 6d.

Ingelow.—Works by JEAN INGELOW

POETICAL WORKS. 2 vols. Fcp. 8vo., 12s.

LYRICAL AND OTHER POEMS. Selected from the Writings of JEAN INGELOW. Fcp. 8vo., 2s. 6d.; cloth plain, 3s. cloth gilt.

Kendall.—SONGS FROM DREAMLAND. By MAY KENDALL. Fcp. 8vo., 5s. net.

Lang.—Works by ANDREW LANG.

BAN AND ARRIÈRE BAN. A Rally of Fugitive Rhymes Fcp. 8vo., 5s. net.

GRASS OF PARNASSUS. Fcp. 8vo., 2s. 6d. net.

BALLADS OF BOOKS. Edited by ANDREW LANG. Fcp. 8vo., 6s.

THE BLUE POETRY BOOK. Edited by ANDREW LANG. With 12 Plates and 88 Illustrations in the Text by H. J. FORD and LANCELOT SPEED. Crown 8vo., 6s.

Special Edition, printed on Indian paper. With Notes, but without Illustrations. Crown 8vo., 7s. 6d.

Lecky.—POEMS. By W. E. H. LECKY. Fcp. 8vo., 5s.

Peek. — Works by HEDLEY PEEK (FRANK LEYTON).

SKELETON LEAVES : Poems. With a Dedicatory Poem to the late Hon. Roden Noel. Fcp. 8vo., 2s. 6d. net.

THE SHADOWS OF THE LAKE, and other Poems. Fcp. 8vo., 2s. 6d. net.

Lytton.—Works by THE EARL OF LYTTON (OWEN MEREDITH).

MARAH. Fcp. 8vo., 6s. 6d.

KING POPPY : a Fantasia. With 1 Plate and Design on Title-Page by Sir ED. BURNE-JONES, A.R.A. Crown 8vo., 10s. 6d.

THE WANDERER. Cr. 8vo., 10s. 6d.

LUCILE. Crown 8vo., 10s. 6d.

SELECTED POEMS. Cr. 8vo., 10s. 6d.

Poetry and the Drama—*continued*.

Macaulay.—LAYS OF ANCIENT ROME, &c. By Lord MACAULAY.
Illustrated by G. SCHARF. Fcp. 4to., 10s. 6d.
——————— Bijou Edition. 18mo., 2s. 6d., gilt top.
——————— Popular Edition. Fcp. 4to., 6d. sewed, 1s. cloth.
Illustrated by J. R. WEGUELIN. Crown 8vo., 3s. 6d.
Annotated Edition. Fcp. 8vo., 1s. sewed, 1s. 6d. cloth.

Murray.—(ROBERT F.), Author of 'The Scarlet Gown'. His Poems, with a Memoir by ANDREW LANG. Fcp. 8vo., 5s. net.

Nesbit.—LAYS AND LEGENDS. By E. NESBIT (Mrs. HUBERT BLAND). First Series. Crown 8vo., 3s. 6d. Second Series, with Portrait. Crown 8vo., 5s.

Piatt.—Works by SARAH PIATT.
POEMS. With portrait of the Author. 2 vols. Crown 8vo., 10s.
AN ENCHANTED CASTLE, AND OTHER POEMS: Pictures, Portraits and People in Ireland. Crown 8vo., 3s. 6d.

Piatt.—Works by JOHN JAMES PIATT.
IDYLS AND LYRICS OF THE OHIO VALLEY. Crown 8vo., 5s.
LITTLE NEW WORLD IDYLS. Cr. 8vo., 5s.

Rhoades.—TERESA AND OTHER POEMS. By JAMES RHOADES. Crown 8vo., 3s. 6d.

Riley.—Works by JAMES WHITCOMB RILEY.
OLD FASHIONED ROSES: Poems. 12mo., 5s.
POEMS HERE AT HOME. Fcap. 8vo., 6s. net.

Shakespeare.—BOWDLER'S FAMILY SHAKESPEARE. With 36 Woodcuts. 1 vol. 8vo., 14s. Or in 6 vols. Fcp. 8vo., 21s.
THE SHAKESPEARE BIRTHDAY BOOK. By MARY F. DUNBAR. 32mo., 1s. 6d.

Sturgis.—A BOOK OF SONG. By JULIAN STURGIS. 16mo., 5s.

Works of Fiction, Humour, &c.

Alden.—AMONG THE FREAKS. By W. L. Alden. With 55 Illustrations by J. F. SULLIVAN and FLORENCE K. UPTON. Crown 8vo, 3s. 6d.

Anstey.—Works by F. ANSTEY, Author of 'Vice Versâ'.
THE BLACK POODLE, and other Stories. Crown 8vo., 2s. boards, 2s. 6d. cloth.
VOCES POPULI. Reprinted from 'Punch'. First Series. With 20 Illustrations by J. BERNARD PARTRIDGE. Cr. 8vo., 3s. 6d.
THE TRAVELLING COMPANIONS. Reprinted from 'Punch'. With 25 Illus. by J. B. PARTRIDGE. Post 4to., 5s.
THE MAN FROM BLANKLEY'S: a Story in Scenes, and other Sketches. With 24 Illustrations by J. BERNARD PARTRIDGE. Fcp. 4to., 6s.

Arnold.—THE STORY OF ULLA, and other Tales. By EDWIN LESTER ARNOLD. Crown 8vo., 6s.

Astor.—A JOURNEY IN OTHER WORLDS, a Romance of the Future. By JOHN JACOB ASTOR. With 10 Illustrations. Cr. 8vo., 6s.

Baker.—BY THE WESTERN SEA. By JAMES BAKER, Author of 'John Westacott'. Crown 8vo., 3s. 6d.

Beaconsfield.—Works by the Earl of BEACONSFIELD.
NOVELS AND TALES. Cheap Edition Complete in 11 vols. Cr. 8vo., 1s. 6d. each.

Vivian Grey.	Henrietta Temple.
The Young Duke, &c.	Venetia. Tancred.
Alroy, Ixion, &c.	Coningsby. Sybil
Contarini Fleming, &c.	Lothair. Endymion

NOVELS AND TALES. The Hughenden Edition. With 2 Portraits and Vignettes. 11 vols. Cr. 8vo., 42s.

Boulton.—JOSEPHINE CREWE. By HELEN M. BOULTON. Cr. 8vo., 6s.

Carmichael.—POEMS. By JENNINGS CARMICHAEL (Mrs. FRANCIS MULLIS). Crown 8vo. 6s. net.

Clegg.—DAVID'S LOOM: a Story of Rochdale life in the early years of the Nineteenth Century. By JOHN TRAFFORD CLEGG. Crown 8vo. 2s. 6d.

Works of Fiction, Humour, &c.—*continued.*

Deland.—PHILIP AND HIS WIFE. By MARGARET DELAND, Author of 'John Ward'. Cr. 8vo., 6s.

Dougall.—Works by L. DOUGALL.
BEGGARS ALL. Crown 8vo., 3s. 6d.
WHAT NECESSITY KNOWS. Crown 8vo., 6s.

Doyle.—Works by A. CONAN DOYLE.
MICAH CLARKE: a Tale of Monmouth's Rebellion. With 10 Illustrations. Cr. 8vo., 3s. 6d.
THE CAPTAIN OF THE POLESTAR, and other Tales. Cr. 8vo., 3s. 6d.
THE REFUGEES: a Tale of the Huguenots. With 25 Illustrations. Crown 8vo., 3s. 6d.
THE STARK-MUNRO LETTERS. Cr. 8vo., 6s.

Farrar.—Works by F. W. FARRAR, Dean of Canterbury.
DARKNESS AND DAWN: or, Scenes in the Days of Nero. An Historic Tale. Cr. 8vo., 7s. 6d.
GATHERING CLOUDS: a Tale of the Days of St. Chrysostom. 2 vols. 8vo, 28s.

Froude.—THE TWO CHIEFS OF DUNBOY: an Irish Romance of the Last Century. By J. A. FROUDE. Cr. 8vo., 3s. 6d.

Fowler.—THE YOUNG PRETENDERS. A Story of Child Life. By EDITH H. FOWLER. With 12 Illustrations by PHILIP BURNE-JONES. Crown 8vo., 6s.

Gerard.—AN ARRANGED MARRIAGE. By DOROTHEA GERARD. Cr. 8vo., 6s.

Gilkes.—THE THING THAT HATH BEEN: or, a Young Man's Mistake. By A. H. GILKES, M.A. Crown 8vo., 6s.

Haggard.—Works by H. RIDER HAGGARD.
SHE. 32 Illustrations. Cr. 8vo., 3s. 6d.
ALLAN QUATERMAIN. With 31 Illustrations. Crown 8vo., 3s. 6d.
MAIWA'S REVENGE. Crown 8vo., 1s. boards; 1s. 6d. cloth.
COLONEL QUARITCH, V.C. Cr. 8vo., 3s. 6d.
CLEOPATRA. With 29 Illustrations Crown 8vo., 3s. 6d.
BEATRICE. Cr. 8vo., 3s. 6d.
ERIC BRIGHTEYES. With 51 Illustrations. Cr. 8vo., 3s. 6d.
HEART OF THE WORLD. With 15 Illustrations, Crown 8vo., 6s.
JOAN HASTE. With 20 Illustrations. Cr. 8vo., 6s.
THE PEOPLE OF THE MIST. With 16 Illustrations. Crown 8vo., 6s.
MONTEZUMA'S DAUGHTER. With 24 Illustrations. Crown 8vo., 3s. 6d.

Haggard.—Works by H. RIDER HAGGARD—*continued.*
NADA THE LILY. With 23 Illustrations. Cr. 8vo., 3s. 6d.
ALLAN'S WIFE. With 34 Illustrations. Crown 8vo., 3s. 6d.
THE WITCH'S HEAD. With 16 Illustrations. Crown 8vo., 3s. 6d.
MR. MEESON'S WILL. With 16 Illustrations. Crown 8vo., 3s. 6d.
DAWN. With 16 Illustrations. Crown 8vo., 3s. 6d.

Haggard and Lang.—THE WORLD'S DESIRE. By H. RIDER HAGGARD and ANDREW LANG. With 27 Illustrations by M. GREIFFENHAGEN. Cr. 8vo., 3s. 6d.

Harte.— IN THE CARQUINEZ WOODS, and other Stories. By BRET HARTE. Cr. 8vo., 3s. 6d.

Hornung.—THE UNBIDDEN GUEST. By E. W. HORNUNG. Cr. 8vo., 3s. 6d.

Jewett.—THE LIFE OF NANCY, AND OTHER STORIES. By SARAH ORNE JEWETT. Crown 8vo., 6s.

Lang.—A MONK OF FIFE: a Romance of the Days of Jeanne D'Arc. By ANDREW LANG. With Illustrations and Initial Letters by SELWYN IMAGE. Crown 8vo, 6s.

Lemon.—MATTHEW FURTH. By IDA LEMON. Crown 8vo., 6s.

Lyall.—Works by EDNA LYALL.
THE AUTOBIOGRAPHY OF A SLANDER. Fcp. 8vo., 1s. sewed.
Presentation Edition. With 20 Illustrations. Cr. 8vo., 2s. 6d. net.
DOREEN: The Story of a Singer. Cr. 8vo., 6s.

Matthews.—HIS FATHER'S SON: a Novel of the New York Stock Exchange. By BRANDER MATTHEWS. With Illus. Cr. 8vo., 6s.

Melville.—Works by G. J. WHYTE MELVILLE.

The Gladiators.	Holmby House.
The Interpreter.	Kate Coventry.
Good for Nothing.	Digby Grand.
The Queen's Maries.	General Bounce.

Cr. 8vo., 1s. 6d. each.

Oliphant.—Works by Mrs. OLIPHANT.
OLD MR. TREDGOLD. Cr. 8vo., 6s.
MADAM. Cr. 8vo., 1s. 6d.
IN TRUST. Cr. 8vo., 1s. 6d.

Payn.—Works by JAMES PAYN.
THE LUCK OF THE DARRELLS. Cr. 8vo., 1s. 6d.
THICKER THAN WATER. Cr. 8vo., 1s. 6d.

Works of Fiction, Humour, &c.—*continued.*

Phillipps-Wolley.—SNAP: a Legend of the Lone Mountain. By C. PHILLIPPS-WOLLEY. With 13 Illustrations by H. G. WILLINK. Cr. 8vo., 3*s*. 6*d*.

Prince.—THE STORY OF CHRISTINE ROCHEFORT. By HELEN CHOATE PRINCE. Crown 8vo., 6*s*.

Quintana.—THE CID CAMPEADOR: an Historical Romance. By D. ANTONIO DE TRUEBA Y LA QUINTANA. Translated from the Spanish by Henry J. Gill, M.A., T.C.D. Crown 8vo, 6*s*.

Rhoscomyl.—Works by OWEN RHOSCOMYL.
THE JEWEL OF YNYS GALON. Crown 8vo., 6*s*.
BATTLEMENT AND TOWER: a Romance. Crown 8vo., 6*s*.

Robertson.—NUGGETS IN THE DEVIL'S PUNCH BOWL, and other Australian Tales. By ANDREW ROBERTSON. Cr. 8vo., 3*s*. 6*d*.

Sewell.—Works by ELIZABETH M. SEWELL.
A Glimpse of the World. | Amy Herbert.
Laneton Parsonage. | Cleve Hall.
Margaret Percival. | Gertrude.
Katharine Ashton. | Home Life.
The Earl's Daughter. | After Life.
The Experience of Life. | Ursula. Ivors.
Cr. 8vo., 1*s*. 6*d*. each cloth plain. 2*s*. 6*d*. each cloth extra, gilt edges.

Stevenson.—Works by ROBERT LOUIS STEVENSON.
STRANGE CASE OF DR. JEKYLL AND MR. HYDE. Fcp. 8vo., 1*s*. sewed. 1*s*. 6*d*. cloth.
THE STRANGE CASE OF DR. JEKYLL AND MR. HYDE; with Other Fables. Crown 8vo., 6*s*. net.
THE DYNAMITER. Cr. 8vo., 3*s*. 6*d*.

Stevenson and Osbourne.—THE WRONG BOX. By ROBERT LOUIS STEVENSON and LLOYD OSBOURNE. Cr. 8vo., 3*s*. 6*d*.

Suttner.—LAY DOWN YOUR ARMS *Die Waffen Nieder:* The Autobiography of Martha Tilling. By BERTHA VON SUTTNER. Translated by T. HOLMES. Cr. 8vo., 1*s*. 6*d*.

Trollope.—Works by ANTHONY TROLLOPE.
THE WARDEN. Cr. 8vo., 1*s*. 6*d*.
BARCHESTER TOWERS. Cr. 8vo., 1*s*. 6*d*.

TRUE, A, RELATION OF THE TRAVELS AND PERILOUS ADVENTURES OF MATHEW DUDGEON, Gentleman : Wherein is truly set down the Manner of his Taking, the Long Time of his Slavery in Algiers, and Means of his Delivery. Written by Himself, and now for the first time printed Cr. 8vo., 5*s*.

Walford.—Works by L. B. WALFORD.
Mr. SMITH : a Part of his Life. Crown 8vo., 2*s*. 6*d*.
THE BABY'S GRANDMOTHER. Crown 8vo., 2*s*. 6*d*.
COUSINS. Crown 8vo. 2*s*. 6*d*.
TROUBLESOME DAUGHTERS. Crown 8vo., 2*s*. 6*d*.
PAULINE. Crown 8vo. 2*s*. 6*d*.
DICK NETHERBY. Crown 8vo., 2*s*. 6*d*.
THE HISTORY OF A WEEK. Crown 8vo. 2*s*. 6*d*.
A STIFF-NECKED GENERATION. Crown 8vo. 2*s*. 6*d*.
NAN, and other Stories. Cr. 8vo., 2*s*. 6*d*.
THE MISCHIEF OF MONICA. Crown 8vo., 2*s*. 6*d*.
THE ONE GOOD GUEST. Cr. 8vo. 2*s*. 6*d*.
'PLOUGHED,' and other Stories. Crown 8vo., 6*s*.
THE MATCHMAKER. Cr. 8vo., 6*s*.

West.—Works by B. B. WEST.
HALF-HOURS WITH THE MILLIONAIRES : Showing how much harder it is to spend a million than to make it. Cr. 8vo., 6*s*.
SIR SIMON VANDERPETTER, AND MINDING HIS ANCESTORS. Two Reformations. Crown 8vo., 5*s*.
A FINANCIAL ATONEMENT. Cr. 8vo., 6*s*.

Weyman.—Works by S. J. WEYMAN.
THE HOUSE OF THE WOLF. Cr. 8vo., 3*s*. 6*d*.
A GENTLEMAN OF FRANCE. Cr. 8vo., 6*s*.
THE RED COCKADE. Cr. 8vo., 6*s*.

Popular Science (Natural History, &c.).

Butler.—OUR HOUSEHOLD INSECTS. An Account of the Insect-Pests found in Dwelling-Houses. By EDWARD A. BUTLER, B.A., B.Sc. (Lond.). With 113 Illustrations. Crown 8vo., 3*s*. 6*d*.

Clodd.—A PRIMER OF EVOLUTION: being a Popular Abridged Edition of ' The Story of Creation '. By EDWARD CLODD. With Illus. Fcp. 8vo., 1*s*. 6*d*.

Furneaux.—Works by W. FURNEAUX.
BUTTERFLIES AND MOTHS (British). With 12 coloured Plates and 241 Illustrations in the Text. Crown 8vo., 12*s*. 6*d*.
THE OUTDOOR WORLD ; or, The Young Collector's Handbook. With 18 Plates, 16 of which are coloured, and 549 Illustrations in the Text. Crown 8vo., 7*s*. 6*d*.

Popular Science (Natural History, &c.).

Graham.—COUNTRY PASTIMES FOR BOYS. By P. ANDERSON GRAHAM. With numerous Illustrations from Drawings and Photographs. Crown 8vo., 6s.

Hartwig.—Works by Dr. GEORGE HARTWIG.

THE SEA AND ITS LIVING WONDERS. With 12 Plates and 303 Woodcuts. 8vo., 7s. net.

THE TROPICAL WORLD. With 8 Plates and 172 Woodcuts. 8vo., 7s. net.

THE POLAR WORLD. With 3 Maps, 8 Plates and 85 Woodcuts. 8vo., 7s. net.

THE SUBTERRANEAN WORLD. With 3 Maps and 80 Woodcuts. 8vo., 7s. net.

THE AERIAL WORLD. With Map, 8 Plates and 60 Woodcuts. 8vo., 7s net.

Hayward.—BIRD NOTES. By the late IANE MARY HAYWARD. Edited by EMMA HUBBARD. With Frontispiece and 15 Illustrations by G. E. LODGE. Cr. 8vo., 6s.

Helmholtz.—POPULAR LECTURES ON SCIENTIFIC SUBJECTS. By HERMANN VON HELMHOLTZ. With 68 Woodcuts. 2 vols. Crown 8vo., 3s. 6d. each.

Hudson.—BRITISH BIRDS. By W. H. HUDSON, C.M.Z.S. With a Chapter on Structure and Classification by FRANK E. BEDDARD, F.R.S. With 17 Plates (8 of which are Coloured), and over 100 Illustrations in the Text. Crown 8vo., 12s. 6d.

Proctor.—Works by RICHARD A. PROCTOR.

LIGHT SCIENCE FOR LEISURE HOURS. Familiar Essays on Scientific Subjects. 3 vols. Crown 8vo., 5s. each.

CHANCE AND LUCK: a Discussion of the Laws of Luck, Coincidence, Wagers, Lotteries and the Fallacies of Gambling, &c. Cr. 8vo., 2s. boards, 2s. 6d. cloth.

ROUGH WAYS MADE SMOOTH. Familiar Essays on Scientific Subjects. Silver Library Edition. Cr. 8vo., 3s. 6d.

PLEASANT WAYS IN SCIENCE. Cr. 8vo., 5s. Silver Library Edition. Crown 8vo., 3s. 6d.

Proctor. — Works by RICHARD A. PROCTOR—continued.

THE GREAT PYRAMID, OBSERVATORY, TOMB AND TEMPLE. With Illustrations. Crown 8vo., 5s.

NATURE STUDIES. By R. A. PROCTOR, GRANT ALLEN, A. WILSON, T. FOSTER and E. CLODD. Crown 8vo., 5s. Sil. Lib. Ed. Cr. 8vo., 3s. 6d.

LEISURE READINGS. By R. A. PROCTOR, E. CLODD, A. WILSON, T. FOSTER, and A. C. RANYARD. Cr. 8vo., 3s. 6d.

Stanley.—A FAMILIAR HISTORY OF BIRDS. By E. STANLEY, D.D., formerly Bishop of Norwich. With Illustrations. Cr. 8vo., 3s. 6d.

Wood.—Works by the Rev. J. G. WOOD.

HOMES WITHOUT HANDS: a Description of the Habitation of Animals, classed according to the Principle of Construction. With 140 Illustrations. 8vo., 7s. net.

INSECTS AT HOME: a Popular Account of British Insects, their Structure, Habits and Transformations. With 700 Illustrations. 8vo., 7s. net.

INSECTS ABROAD: a Popular Account of Foreign Insects, their Structure, Habits and Transformations. With 600 Illustrations. 8vo., 7s. net.

BIBLE ANIMALS: a Description of every Living Creature mentioned in the Scriptures. With 112 Illustrations. 8vo., 7s. net.

PETLAND REVISITED. With 33 Illustrations. Cr. 8vo., 3s. 6d.

OUT OF DOORS; a Selection of Original Articles on Practical Natural History. With 11 Illustrations. Cr. 8vo., 3s. 6d.

STRANGE DWELLINGS: a Description of the Habitations of Animals, abridged from 'Homes without Hands'. With 60 Illustrations. Cr. 8vo., 3s. 6d.

Works of Reference.

Longmans' GAZETTEER OF THE WORLD. Edited by GEORGE G. CHISHOLM, M.A., B.Sc., Fellow of the Royal Geographical and Statistical Societies. Imp. 8vo. £2 2s. cloth, £2 12s. 6d. half-morocco.

Maunder's (Samuel) Treasuries.
BIOGRAPHICAL TREASURY. With Supplement brought down to 1889. By Rev. JAMES WOOD. Fcp. 8vo., 6s.

TREASURY OF NATURAL HISTORY: or, Popular Dictionary of Zoology. With 900 Woodcuts. Fcp. 8vo., 6s.

TREASURY OF GEOGRAPHY, Physical, Historical, Descriptive, and Political. With 7 Maps and 16 Plates. Fcp. 8vo., 6s.

THE TREASURY OF BIBLE KNOWLEDGE. By the Rev. J. AYRE, M.A. With 5 Maps, 15 Plates, and 300 Woodcuts. Fcp. 8vo., 6s.

HISTORICAL TREASURY: Outlines of Universal History, Separate Histories of all Nations. Fcp. 8vo., 6s.

Maunder's (Samuel) Treasuries
—*continued.*
TREASURY OF KNOWLEDGE AND LIBRARY OF REFERENCE. Comprising an English Dictionary and Grammar, Universal Gazeteer, Classical Dictionary, Chronology, Law Dictionary, &c. Fcp. 8vo., 6s.

SCIENTIFIC AND LITERARY TREASURY. Fcp. 8vo., 6s.

THE TREASURY OF BOTANY. Edited by J. LINDLEY, F.R.S., and T. MOORE, F.L.S. With 274 Woodcuts and 20 Steel Plates. 2 vols. Fcp. 8vo., 12s.

Roget.--THESAURUS OF ENGLISH WORDS AND PHRASES. Classified and Arranged so as to Facilitate the Expression of Ideas and assist in Literary Composition. By PETER MARK ROGET, M.D., F.R.S. Crown 8vo., 10s. 6d.

Willich.—POPULAR TABLES for giving information for ascertaining the value or Lifehold, Leasehold, and Church Property, the Public Funds, &c. By CHARLES M. WILLICH. Edited by H. BENCE JONES. Crown 8vo., 10s. 6d.

Children's Books.

Bird.—Works by ROBERT BIRD.
JOSEPH THE DREAMER. Cr. 8vo., 5s.
JESUS, THE CARPENTER OF NAZARETH. Crown 8vo, 5s.
To be had also in Two Parts, 2s. 6d. each.
Part. I.—GALILEE AND THE LAKE OF GENNESARET.
Part II.—JERUSALEM AND THE PERÆA.
A CHILD'S RELIGION. Crown 8vo., 2s.
Crake.—Works by Rev. A. D. CRAKE.
EDWY THE FAIR; or, the First Chronicle of Æscendune. Crown 8vo., 2s. 6d.
ALFGAR THE DANE: or, the Second Chronicle of Æscendune. Cr. 8vo., 2s. 6d.
THE RIVAL HEIRS: being the Third and Last Chronicle of Æscendune. Cr. 8vo., 2s. 6d.
THE HOUSE OF WALDERNE. A Tale of the Cloister and the Forest in the Days of the Barons' Wars. Crown 8vo., 2s. 6d.
BRIAN FITZ-COUNT. A Story of Wallingford Castle and Dorchester Abbey. Cr. 8vo., 2s. 6d.
Lang.—Works edited by ANDREW LANG.
THE BLUE FAIRY BOOK. With 138 Illustrations. Crown 8vo., 6s.
THE RED FAIRY BOOK. With 100 Illustrations. Cr. 8vo., 6s.
THE GREEN FAIRY BOOK. With 101 Illustrations. Crown 8vo., 6s.
THE YELLOW FAIRY BOOK. With 104 Illustrations. Crown 8vo., 6s.
THE BLUE POETRY BOOK. With 100 Illustrations. Crown 8vo., 6s.

Lang.—Works edited by ANDREW LANG
—*continued.*
THE BLUE POETRY BOOK. School Edition, without Illustrations. Fcp. 8vo., 2s. 6d.
THE TRUE STORY BOOK. With 66 Illustrations. Crown 8vo., 6s.
THE RED TRUE STORY BOOK. With 100 Illustrations. Crown 8vo., 6s.
Meade.—Works by L. T. MEADE.
DADDY'S BOY. Illustrated. Crown 8vo., 3s. 6d.
DEB AND THE DUCHESS. Illustrated. Crown 8vo., 3s. 6d.
THE BERESFORD PRIZE. Crown 8vo., 3s. 6d.
HOUSE OF SURPRISES. Crown 8vo. 3s. 6d.
Molesworth.—Works by Mrs. MOLESWORTH.
SILVERTHORNS. Illustrated. Cr. 8vo., 5s.
NEIGHBOURS. Illus. Crown 8vo., 2s. 6d.
Stevenson.—A CHILD'S GARDEN OF VERSES. By ROBERT LOUIS STEVENSON. Small fcp. 8vo., 5s.
Upton.—THE ADVENTURES OF TWO DUTCH DOLLS AND A 'GOLLIWOGG'. Illustrated by FLORENCE K. UPTON, with Words by BERTHA UPTON. With 31 Coloured Plates and numerous Illustrations in the Text. Oblong 4to., 6s.
Wordsworth.—THE SNOW GARDEN, and other Fairy Tales for Children. By ELIZABETH WORDSWORTH. With Illustrations by TREVOR HADDON. Cr. 8vo., 5s.

Longmans' Series of Books for Girls.
Crown 8vo., price 2s. 6d. each

ATELIER (THE) DU LYS: or an Art Student in the Reign of Terror.
BY THE SAME AUTHOR.

Mademoiselle Mori. A Chi'd of the Revolu-
That Child. tion.
Under a Cloud. | Hester's Venture.
The Fiddler of | In the Olden Time.
Lugau. | The Younger Sister.

THE THIRD MISS ST. QUENTIN. By Mrs. MOLESWORTH.
THE PALACE IN THE GARDEN. Illustrated. By Mrs. MOLESWORTH.
ATHERSTONE PRIORY. By L. N. COMYN.
THE STORY OF A SPRING MORNING, &c. By Mrs. MOLESWORTH. Illustrated.

NEIGHBOURS. By Mrs. MOLESWORTH.
VERY YOUNG; and QUITE ANOTHER STORY. By JEAN INGELOW.
CAN THIS BE LOVE? By Louis A. Parr.
KEITH DERAMORE. By the Author of ' Miss Molly '.
SIDNEY. By MARGARET DELAND.
LAST WORDS TO GIRLS ON LIFE AT SCHOOL AND AFTER SCHOOL. By Mrs. W. GREY.

STRAY THOUGHTS FOR GIRLS. By LUCY H. M. SOULSBY. 16mo., 1s. 6d. net.

The Silver Library.
CROWN 8vo. 3s. 6d. EACH VOLUME.

Arnold's (Sir Edwin) Seas and Lands. With 71 Illustrations. 3s. 6d.
Bagehot's (W.) Biographical Studies. 3s. 6d.
Bagehot's (W.) Economic Studies. 3s. 6d.
Bagehot's (W.) Literary Studies. 3 vols. 3s. 6d. each. With Portrait.
Baker's (Sir S. W.) Eight Years in Ceylon. With 6 Illustrations. 3s. 6d.
Baker's (Sir S. W.) Rifle and Hound in Ceylon. With 6 Illustrations. 3s. 6d.
Baring-Gould's (Rev. S.) Curious Myths of the Middle Ages. 3s. 6d.
Baring-Gould's (Rev. S.) Origin and Development of Religious Belief. 2 vols. 3s. 6d. each.
Becker's (Prof.) Gallus: or, Roman Scenes in the Time of Augustus. Illus. 3s. 6d.
Becker's (Prof.) Charicles: or, Illustrations of the Private Life of the Ancient Greeks. Illustrated. 3s. 6d.
Bent's (J. T.) The Ruined Cities of Mashoonland: being a Record of Excavation and Exploration in 1891. With 117 Illustrations. 3s. 6d.
Brassey's (Lady) A Voyage in the 'Sunbeam'. With 66 Illustrations. 3s. 6d.
Butler's (Edward A.) Our Household Insects: an Account of the Insect-Pests found in Dwelling-Houses. With 7 Plates and 113 Illustrations in the Text.
Clodd's (E.) Story of Creation: a Plain Account of Evolution. With 77 Illustrations. 3s. 6d.
Conybeare (Rev. W. J.) and Howson's (Very Rev. J. S.) Life and Epistles of St. Paul. 46 Illustrations. 3s. 6d.
Dougall's (L.) Beggars All; a Novel. 3s. 6d.
Doyle's (A. Conan) Micah Clarke: a Tale of Monmouth's Rebellion. 10 Illus. 3s. 6d.
Doyle's (A. Conan) The Captain of the Polestar, and other Tales. 3s. 6d.
Doyle's (A. Conan) The Refugees: A Tale of The Huguenots. With 25 Illustrations, 3s. 6d.

Froude's (J. A.) Short Studies on Great Subjects. 4 vols. 3s. 6d. each.
Froude's (J. A.) Cæsar: a Sketch. 3s. 6d.
Froude's (J. A.) Thomas Carlyle a History of his Life.
1795-1835. 2 vols. 7s.
1834-1881. 2 vols. 7s.
Froude's (J. A.) The Two Chiefs of Dunboy: an Irish Romance of the Last Century. 3s. 6d.
Froude's (J. A.) The History of England, from the Fall of Wolsey to the Defeat of the Spanish Armada. 12 vols. 3s. 6d. each.
Froude's (J. A.) The English in Ireland. 3 vols. 10s. 6d.
Froude's (J. A.) The Spanish Story of the Armada, and other Essays. 3s. 6d.
Gleig's (Rev. G. R.) Life of the Duke of Wellington. With Portrait. 3s. 6d.
Haggard's (H. R.) She: A History of Adventure. 32 Illustrations. 3s. 6d.
Haggard's (H. R.) Allan Quatermain. With 20 Illustrations. 3s. 6d.
Haggard's (H. R.) Colonel Quaritch, V.C.: a Tale of Country Life. 3s. 6d.
Haggard's (H. R.) Cleopatra. With 29 Full-page Illustrations. 3s. 6d.
Haggard's (H. R.) Eric Brighteyes. With 51 Illustrations. 3s. 6d.
Haggard's (H. R.) Beatrice. 3s. 6d.
Haggard's (H. R.) Allan's Wife. With 34 Illustrations. 3s. 6d.
Haggard's (H. R.) The Witch's Head. With Illustrations. 3s. 6d.
Haggard's (H. R.) Mr. Meeson's Will. With Illustrations. 3s. 6d.
Haggard's (H. R.) Dawn. With 16 Illustrations. 3s. 6d.
Haggard's (H. R.) and Lang's (A.) The World's Desire. With 27 Illus. 3s. 6d.
Haggard's (H. R.) Montezuma's Daughter. With 25 Illustrations.

The Silver Library—*continued.*

Haggard's (H. R.) Nada the Lily. With Illustrations by C. H. M. KERR. 3*s.* 6*d.*

Harte's (Bret) In the Carquinez Woods, and other Stories. 3*s.* 6*d.*

Helmholtz's (Hermann von) Popular Lectures on Scientific Subjects. With 68 Woodcuts. 2 vols. 3*s.* 6*d.* each.

Hornung's (E. W.) The Unbidden Guest. 3*s.* 6*d.*

Howitt's (W.) Visits to Remarkable Places. 80 Illustrations. 3*s.* 6*d.*

Jefferies' (R.) The Story of My Heart: My Autobiography. With Portrait. 3*s.* 6*d.*

Jefferies' (R.) Field and Hedgerow. With Portrait. 3*s.* 6*d.*

Jefferies' (R.) Red Deer. 17 Illus. 3*s.* 6*d.*

Jefferies' (R.) Wood Magic: a Fable. 3*s.* 6*d.*

Jefferies' (R. The Toilers of the Field. With Portrait from the Bust in Salisbury Cathedral. 3*s.* 6*d.*

Knight's (E. F.) The Cruise of the 'Alerte': a Search for Treasure on the Desert Island of Trinidad. 2 Maps and 23 Illustrations. 3*s.* 6*d.*

Knight's (E. F.) Where Three Empires Meet: a Narrative of Recent Travel in Kashmir, Western Tibet, etc. With a Map and 54 Illust. 3*s.* 6*d.*

Lang's (A.) Angling Sketches. 20 Illus. 3*s.* 6*d.*

Lang's (A.) Custom and Myth: Studies of Early Usage and Belief. 3*s.* 6*d.*

Lang's (A.) Cock Lane and Common-Sense. With a New Preface.

Lees (J. A.) and Clutterbuck's (W.J.) B.C. 1887, A Ramble in British Columbia. With Maps and 75 Illustrations. 3*s.* 6*d.*

Macaulay's (Lord) Essays and Lays of Ancient Rome. With Portrait and Illustrations. 3*s.* 6*d.*

Macleod's (H. D.) The Elements of Banking. 3*s.* 6*d.*

Marshman's (J. C.) Memoirs of Sir Henry Havelock. 3*s.* 6*d.*

Max Müller's (F.) India, what can it teach us? 3*s.* 6*d.*

Max Müller's (F.) Introduction to the Science of Religion. 3*s.* 6*d.*

Merivale's (Dean) History of the Romans under the Empire. 8 vols. 3*s.* 6*d.* ea.

Mill's (J. S.) Political Economy. 3*s.* 6*d.*

Mill's (J. S.) System of Logic. 3*s.* 6*d.*

Milner's (Geo.) Country Pleasures. 3*s.* 6*d.*

Nansen's (F.) The First Crossing of Greenland. With Illustrations and a Map. 3*s.* 6*d.*

Phillipps-Wolley's (C.) Snap: a Legend of the Lone Mountain. With 13 Illustrations. 3*s.* 6*d.*

Proctor's (R. A.) The Orbs Around Us. Essays on the Moon and Planets, Meteors and Comets, the Sun and Coloured Pairs of Suns. 3*s.* 6*d.*

Proctor's (R. A.) The Expanse of Heaven. Essays on the Wonders of the Firmament. 3*s.* 6*d.*

Proctor's (R. A.) Other Worlds than Ours. 3*s.* 6*d.*

Proctor's (R. A.) Rough Ways made Smooth. 3*s.* 6*d.*

Proctor's (R. A.) Pleasant Ways in Science. 3*s.* 6*d.*

Proctor's (R. A.) Myths and Marvels of Astronomy. 3*s.* 6*d.*

Proctor's (R. A.) Nature Studies. 3*s.* 6*d.*

Proctor's (R. A.), Clodd (Edward), &c. Leisure Readings. With Illustrations.

Rossetti's (Maria F.) A Shadow of Dante: an Essay towards studying Himself, his World and his Pilgrimage. 3*s.* 6*d.*

Smith's (R. Bosworth) Carthage and the Carthaginians. 3*s.* 6*d.*

Stanley's (Bishop) Familiar History of Birds. 160 Illustrations. 3*s.* 6*d.*

Stevenson (Robert Louis) and Osbourne's (Lloyd) The Wrong Box. 3*s.* 6*d.*

Stevenson (Robt. Louis) and Stevenson's (Fanny van de Grift) More New Arabian Nights. — The Dynamiter. 3*s.* 6*d.*

Weyman's (Stanley J.) The House of the Wolf: a Romance. 3*s.* 6*d.*

Wood's (Rev. J. G.) Petland Revisited. With 33 Illustrations. 3*s.* 6*d.*

Wood's (Rev. J. G.) Strange Dwellings. With 60 Illustrations. 3*s.* 6*d.*

Wood's (Rev. J. G.) Out of Doors. 11 Illustrations. 3*s.* 6*d.*

Cookery, Domestic Management, &c.

Acton.—MODERN COOKERY. By ELIZA ACTON. With 150 Woodcuts. Fcp. 8vo., 4*s.* 6*d.*

Bull.—Works by THOMAS BULL, M.D.

HINTS TO MOTHERS ON THE MANAGEMENT OF THEIR HEALTH DURING THE PERIOD OF PREGNANCY. Fcp. 8vo., 1*s.* 6*d.*

THE MATERNAL MANAGEMENT OF CHILDREN IN HEALTH AND DISEASE. Fcd. 8vo., 1*s.* 6*d.*

De Salis.—Works by Mrs. DE SALIS.

CAKES AND CONFECTIONS À LA MODE. Fcp. 8vo., 1*s.* 6*d.*

DOGS: a Manual for Amateurs. Fcp. 8vo., 1*s.* 6*d.*

DRESSED GAME AND POULTRY À LA MODE. Fcp. 8vo., 1*s.* 6*d.*

DRESSED VEGETABLES À LA MODE. Fcp. 8vo., 1*s.* 6*d.*

DRINKS À LA MODE. Fcp. 8vo., 1*s.* 6*d.*

ENTRÉES À LA MODE. Fcp. 8vo., 1*s.* 6*d.*

Cookery, Domestic Management, &c.—*continued.*

De Salis.—Works by Mrs. DE SALIS *continued.*

FLORAL DECORATIONS. Fcp. 8vo , 1s. 6d.

GARDENING À LA MODE. Part I. Vegetables, 1s. 6d. ; Part II. Fruits, 1s. 6d.

NATIONAL VIANDS À LA MODE. Fcp. 8vo., 1s. 6d.

NEW-LAID EGGS : Hints for Amateur Poultry Rearers. Fcp. 8vo., 1s. 6d.

OYSTERS À LA MODE. Fcp. 8vo., 1s. 6d.

PUDDINGS AND PASTRY À LA MODE. Fcp. 8vo., 1s. 6d.

SAVOURIES À LA MODE. Fcp. 8vo., 1s. 6d.

SOUPS AND DRESSED FISH À LA MODE. Fcp. 8vo., 1s. 6d.

SWEETS AND SUPPER DISHES À LA MODE. Fcp. 8vo., 1s. 6d.

TEMPTING DISHES FOR SMALL IN-COMES. Fcp. 8vo., 1s. 6d.

WRINKLES AND NOTIONS FOR EVERY HOUSEHOLD. Cr. 8vo., 1s. 6d.

Lear.—MAIGRE COOKERY. By H. L. SIDNEY LEAR. 16mo., 2s.

Poole.—COOKERY FOR THE DIABETIC By W. H. and Mrs. POOLE. With Preface by Dr. PAVY. Fcp. 8vo., 2s. 6d.

Walker.—Works by JANE H. WALKER, L.R.C.P.

A HANDBOOK FOR MOTHERS : being Simple Hints to Women on the Management of their Health during Pregnancy and Confinement, together with Plain Directions as to the Care of Infants. Cr. 8vo., 2s. 6d.

A BOOK FOR EVERY WOMAN. Part 1. The Management of Children in Health and out of Health. Crown 8vo., 2s. 6d.

Miscellaneous and Critical Works.

Allingham.—VARIETIES IN PROSE. By WILLIAM ALLINGHAM. 3 vols. Cr. 8vo, 18s. (Vols. 1 and 2, Rambles, by PATRICIUS WALKER. Vol. 3, Irish Sketches, etc.)

Armstrong.—ESSAYS AND SKETCHES. By EDMUND J. ARMSTRONG. Fcp. 8vo., 5s.

Bagehot.—LITERARY STUDIES. By WALTER BAGEHOT. With Portrait. 3 vols. Crown 8vo., 3s. 6d. each.

Baring-Gould.—CURIOUS MYTHS OF THE MIDDLE AGES. By Rev. S. BARING-GOULD. Crown 8vo., 3s. 6d.

Battye.—PICTURES IN PROSE OF NATURE, WILD SPORT, AND HUMBLE LIFE. By AUBYN TREVOR BATTYE, F.L.S., F.Z.S. Crown 8vo., 6s.

Baynes.—SHAKESPEARE STUDIES, AND OTHER ESSAYS. By the late THOMAS SPENCER BAYNES, LL.B., LL.D. With a biographical Preface by Prof. LEWIS CAMPBELL. Crown 8vo., 7s. 6d.

Boyd ('A. K. H. B.').—Works by A. K. H. BOYD, D.D., LL.D. *And see MISCELLANEOUS THEOLO-GICAL WORKS, p. 24.*

AUTUMN HOLIDAYS OF A COUNTRY PARSON. Crown 8vo., 3s. 6d.

COMMONPLACE PHILOSOPHER. Crown 8vo., 3s. 6d.

CRITICAL ESSAYS OF A COUNTRY PARSON. Crown 8vo., 3s. 6d.

EAST COAST DAYS AND MEMORIES. Crown 8vo., 3s. 6d.

Boyd ('A. K. H. B.').—Works by A. K. H. BOYD, D.D., LL.D.—*continued.*

LANDSCAPES, CHURCHES AND MORA-LITIES. Crown 8vo., 3s. 6d.

LEISURE HOURS IN TOWN. Crown 8vo., 3s. 6d.

LESSONS OF MIDDLE AGE. Cr. 8vo., 3s. 6d

OUR LITTLE LIFE. Two Series. Cr. 8vo., 3s. 6d. each.

OUR HOMELY COMEDY : AND TRAGEDY. Crown 8vo., 3s. 6d.

RECREATIONS OF A COUNTRY PARSON. Three Series. Cr. 8vo., 3s. 6d. each. Also First Series. Popular Ed. 8vo., 6d.

Butler.—Works by SAMUEL BUTLER.

EREWHON. Cr. 8vo., 5s.

THE FAIR HAVEN. A Work in Defence of the Miraculous Element in our Lord's Ministry. Cr. 8vo., 7s. 6d.

LIFE AND HABIT. An Essay after a Completer View of Evolution. Cr. 8vo., 7s. 6d

EVOLUTION, OLD AND NEW. Cr. 8vo., 10s. 6d.

ALPS AND SANCTUARIES OF PIEDMONT AND CANTON TICINO. Illustrated. Pott 4to., 10s. 6d.

LUCK, OR CUNNING, AS THE MAIN MEANS OF ORGANIC MODIFICATION ? Cr. 8vo., 7s. 6d.

EX VOTO. An Account of the Sacro Monte or New Jerusalem at Varallo-Sesia. Crown 8vo., 10s. 6d.

Miscellaneous and Critical Works —*continued.*

Gwilt.—AN ENCYCLOPÆDIA OF ARCHITECTURE. By JOSEPH GWILT, F.S.A. Illustrated with more than 1100 Engravings on Wood. Revised (1888), with Alterations and Considerable Additions by WYATT PAPWORTH. 8vo., £2 12s. 6d.

Jefferies.—Works by R. JEFFERIES.
FIELD AND HEDGEROW : last Essays. With Portrait. Crown 8vo., 3s. 6d.
THE STORY OF MY HEART: With Portrait and New Preface by C. J. LONGMAN. Crown 8vo., 3s. 6d.
RED DEER. 17 Illusts. Cr. 8vo., 3s. 6d.
THE TOILERS OF THE FIELD. With Portrait. Crown 8vo., 3s. 6d.
WOOD MAGIC. With Frontispiece and Vignette by E. V. B. Cr. 8vo., 3s. 6d.
THOUGHTS FROM THE WRITINGS OF RICHARD JEFFERIES. Selected by H. S. HOOLE WAYLEN. 16mo., 3s. 6d.

Johnson.—THE PATENTEE'S MANUAL: a Treatise on the Law and Practice of Letters Patent. By J. & J. H. JOHNSON, Patent Agents, &c. 8vo., 10s. 6d.

Lang.—Works by ANDREW LANG.
LETTERS TO DEAD AUTHORS. Fcp. 8vo., 2s. 6d. net.
LETTERS ON LITERATURE. Fcp. 8vo., 2s. 6d. net.
BOOKS AND BOOKMEN. With 19 Illustrations. Fcp. 8vo., 2s. 6d. net.
OLD FRIENDS. Fcp. 8vo., 2s. 6d. net.
COCK LANE AND COMMON SENSE. Fcp. 8vo., 3s. 6d.

Laurie.—HISTORICAL SURVEY OF PRE-CHRISTIAN EDUCATION. By S. S. LAURIE, A.M., LL.D. Crown 8vo., 12s.

Leonard.—THE CAMEL: Its Uses and Management. By Major ARTHUR GLYN LEONARD. Royal 8vo., 21s. net.

Macfarren.—LECTURES ON HARMONY. By Sir GEO. A. MACFARREN. 8vo., 12s.

Max Müller.—Works by F. MAX MÜLLER.
INDIA: WHAT CAN IT TEACH US ? Cr. 8vo., 3s. 6d.
CHIPS FROM A GERMAN WORKSHOP.
Vol. I., Recent Essays and Addresses. Cr. 8vo., 6s. 6d. net.
Vol. II., Biographical Essays. Cr. 8vo., 6s. 6d. net.
Vol. III., Essays on Language and Literature. Cr. 8vo., 6s. 6d. net.
Vol. IV., Essays on Mythology and Folk Lore. Crown 8vo., 8s. 6d.

Milner.—Works by GEORGE MILNER.
COUNTRY PLEASURES: the Chronicle of a Year chiefly in a Garden. Cr. 8vo., 3s. 6d.

STUDIES OF NATURE ON THE COAST OF ARRAN. With Illustrations by W. NOEL JOHNSON. Cr. 8vo., 6s. 6d. net.

Poore.—ESSAYS ON RURAL HYGIENE. By GEORGE VIVIAN POORE, M.D., F.R.C.P. With 13 Illustrations. Cr. 8vo., 6s. 6d.

Proctor.—Works by R. A PROCTOR.
STRENGTH AND HAPPINESS. With 9 Illustrations. Crown 8vo., 5s.

STRENGTH: How to get Strong and keep Strong, with Chapters on Rowing and Swimming, Fat, Age, and the Waist. With 9 Illus. Cr. 8vo, 2s.

Richardson.—NATIONAL HEALTH. A Review of the Works of Sir Edwin Chadwick, K.C.B. By Sir B. W. RICHARDSON, M.D. Cr. 8vo., 4s. 6d.

Rossetti.—A SHADOW OF DANTE: being an Essay towards studying Himself, his World, and his Pilgrimage. By MARIA FRANCESCA ROSSETTI. Cr. 8vo., 10s. 6d. Cheap Edition, 3s. 6d.

Solovyoff.—A MODERN PRIESTESS OF ISIS (MADAME BLAVATSKY). Abridged and Translated on Behalf of the Society for Psychical Research from the Russian of VSEVOLOD SERGYEEVICH SOLOVYFF. By WALTER LEAF, Litt. D. With Appendices. Crown 8vo., 6s.

Stevens.—ON THE STOWAGE OF SHIPS AND THEIR CARGOES. With Information regarding Freights, Charter-Parties, &c. By ROBERT WHITE STEVENS, Associate Member of the Institute of Naval Architects. 8vo. 21s.

Van Dyke.—A TEXT-BOOK OF THE HISTORY OF PAINTING. By JOHN C. VAN DYKE, of Rutgers College, U.S. With Frontispiece and 109 Illustrations in the Text. Crown 8vo., 6s.

West.—WILLS, AND HOW NOT TO MAKE THEM. With a Selection of Leading Cases. By B. B. WEST. Fcp. 8vo., 2s. 6d.

Miscellaneous Theological Works.

For Church of England and Roman Catholic Works see MESSRS. LONGMANS & CO.'S
Special Catalogues.

Balfour.—THE FOUNDATIONS OF BE-
LIEF : being Notes Introductory to the
Study of Theology. By the Right Hon.
ARTHUR J. BALFOUR, M.P. 8vo., 12s. 6d.

Boyd.—Works by A. K. H. BOYD, D.D.
COUNSEL AND COMFORT FROM A CITY
PULPIT. Crown 8vo., 3s. 6d.
SUNDAY AFTERNOONS IN THE PARISH
CHURCH OF A SCOTTISH UNIVERSITY
CITY. Crown 8vo., 3s. 6d.
CHANGED ASPECTS OF UNCHANGED
TRUTHS. Crown 8vo., 3s. 6d.
GRAVER THOUGHTS OF A COUNTRY
PARSON. Three Series. Crown 8vo.,
3s. 6d. each.
PRESENT DAY THOUGHTS. Crown 8vo.,
3s. 6d.
SEASIDE MUSINGS. Cr. 8vo., 3s. 6d.
'TO MEET THE DAY' through the
Christian Year ; being a Text of Scrip-
ture, with an Original Meditation and
a Short Selection in Verse for Every
Day. Crown 8vo., 4s. 6d.
OCCASIONAL AND IMMEMORIAL DAYS.
Cr. 8vo., 7s. 6d.

De La Saussaye.—A MANUAL OF
THE SCIENCE OF RELIGION. By Prof.
CHANTEPIE DE LA SAUSSAYE. Crown
8vo., 12s. 6d.

Kalisch.—Works by M. M. KALISCH,
BIBLE STUDIES. Part I. The Pro-
phecies of Balaam. 8vo., 10s. 6d. Part
II. The Book of Jonah. 8vo., 10s. 6d.
COMMENTARY ON THE OLD TESTAMENT :
with a new Translation. Vol. I.
Genesis. 8vo., 18s. Or adapted for the
General Reader. 12s. Vol. II. Exodus.
15s. Or adapted for the General
Reader. 12s. Vol. III. Leviticus, Part
I. 15s. Or adapted for the General
Reader. 8s. Vol. IV. Leviticus, Part
II. 15s. Or adapted for the General
Reader. 8s.

Martineau.—Works by JAMES MAR-
TINEAU, D.D., LL.D.
HOURS OF THOUGHT ON SACRED
THINGS : Sermons. 2 Vols. Crown
8vo. 3s. 6d. each.
ENDEAVOURS AFTER THE CHRISTIAN
LIFE. Discourses. Cr. 8vo., 7s. 6d.
THE SEAT OF AUTHORITY IN RELIGION.
8vo., 14s.
ESSAYS, REVIEWS, AND ADDRESSES. 4
Vols. Crown 8vo., 7s. 6d. each. I.
Personal ; Political. II. Ecclesiastical ;
Historical. III. Theological ; Philo-
sophical. IV. Academical ; Religious.
HOME PRAYERS, with Two Services for
Public Worship. Crown 8vo. 3s. 6d.

Macdonald.—Works by GEORGE MAC-
DONALD, LL.D.
UNSPOKEN SERMONS. Three Series.
Crown 8vo., 3s. 6d. each.
THE MIRACLES OF OUR LORD. Crown
8vo., 3s. 6d.
A BOOK OF STRIFE, IN THE FORM OF
THE DIARY OF AN OLD SOUL : Poems
18mo., 6s.

Max Müller.—Works by F. MAX
MÜLLER.
HIBBERT LECTURES ON THE ORIGIN
AND GROWTH OF RELIGION, as illus-
trated by the Religions of India.
Crown 8vo., 7s. 6d.
INTRODUCTION TO THE SCIENCE OF
RELIGION : Four Lectures delivered at
the Royal Institution. Cr. 8vo., 3s. 6d.
NATURAL RELIGION. The Gifford
Lectures, delivered before the Uni-
versity of Glasgow in 1888. Cr. 8vo.,
10s. 6d.
PHYSICAL RELIGION. The Gifford
Lectures, delivered before the Uni-
versity of Glasgow in 1890. Cr. 8vo.,
10s. 6d.
ANTHROPOLOGICAL RELIGION. The Gif-
ford Lectures, delivered before the
University of Glasgow in 1891. Cr.
8vo., 10s. 6d.
THEOSOPHY OR PSYCHOLOGICAL RELI-
GION. The Gifford Lectures, delivered
before the University of Glasgow in 1892.
Cr. 8vo., 10s. 6d.
THREE LECTURES ON THE VEDANTA
PHILOSOPHY, delivered at the Royal
Institution in March, 1894. 8vo., 5s.

Phillips.—THE TEACHING OF THE VE-
DAS. What Light does it Throw on the
Origin and Development of Religion ?
By MAURICE PHILLIPS, London Mission,
Madras. Crown 8vo., 6s.

Romanes.—THOUGHTS ON RELIGION.
By the late GEORGE J. ROMANES, author
of 'Darwin and After Darwin,' &c.
Crown 8vo, 4s. 6d.

SUPERNATURAL RELIGION : an
Inquiry into the Reality of Divine Revelation. 3 vols. 8vo., 36s.
REPLY (A) TO DR. LIGHTFOOT'S ESSAYS.
By the Author of 'Supernatural Religion'. 8vo., 6s.
THE GOSPEL ACCORDING TO ST. PETER :
a Study. By the Author of 'Supernatural Religion'. 8vo., 6s.

Thom.—A SPIRITUAL FAITH. Ser-
mons. By JOHN HAMILTON THOM.
With a Memorial Preface by JAMES
MARTINEAU, D.D. With Portrait.
Crown 8vo. 5s.

CPSIA information can be obtained at www.ICGtesting.com
Printed in the USA
LVOW011602110112

263398LV00003B/11/A

9 781437 477191